The *Really* Useful Guide Working Smarter Not Harder

Also by Ilyce R. Glink

50 Simple Steps You Can Take to Sell Your Home Faster and for More Money in Any Market

50 Simple Steps You Can Take to Disaster-Proof Your Finances

50 Simple Things You Can Do to Improve Your Personal Finances

100 Questions Every First-Time Home Buyer Should Ask

100 Questions You Should Ask about Your Personal Finances

100 Questions Every Home Seller Should Ask

10 Steps to Home Ownership

The *Really* Useful Guide to Working Smarter, Not Harder

ILYCE R. GLINK

Think
Glink

www.thinkglink.com

Published by Think Glink, Inc., Glencoe, Illinois 60022.

www.ThinkGlink.com

Printed in the United States of America

First Edition

For Sam,
who likes it when stuff is really useful

Contents

Letter from Quill's President   xi

Introduction   xiii

CHAPTER 1 Managing Your Time   1

1. Don't Mistake a Fire for an Inferno   5
2. Avoid the Seven Deadly Time Traps   7
3. Learn How to Prioritize When Everyone's Job
   Is Hot   17
4. Keep on Schedule by Saying No or Later—
   in a Nice Way   19
5. Create Schedules, Set Goals, and Keep
   Everyone Focused   21
6. Don't Rely on Multitasking to Make You More
   Productive   25
7. Learn How to Know When You've Done Enough   28
   Top Tips for Managing Your Time   30

CHAPTER 2 Organizing Your Office   33

8. Create a Filing System That Works for You   37
9. Move Ahead with Advanced Filing Tips   43
10. Organize Your Computer Files   49
11. Use Electronic Reminders   55
    Top Tips for Organizing Your Office   57

CHAPTER 3 Dealing with Customers   59

12. Cultivate Your Customer Base   63

13. Refine Your Customer Service   68

14. Polish Up on Customer Etiquette   72

15. Learn How to Deal with Difficult Customers
    and Clients   76

16. Say Thank You in Creative Ways   79

Top Tips for Improving Customer Service   85

CHAPTER 4 Improving Office Relationships   87

17. Learn How to Motivate Your Colleagues
    and Build a Strong Team   91

18. Take Action to Resolve Conflicts   95

19. Improve Communication by Keeping People
    in the Loop   98

20. Learn How to Deal with a Difficult Boss or
    Colleague   101

21. Make Your Office Mates Feel Appreciated   105

22. Polish Up on Cubicle Etiquette   109

Top Tips for Running a Great Holiday Party   112

CHAPTER 5 Making Your Office Safer and More
Comfortable   115

23. Choose and Use the Right Equipment and Furniture
    for Your Office   121

24. Shed a Little Light on the Subject   129

25. Improve Office Safety and Security   133

Top Tips for Preventing Crime in Your Office   139

CHAPTER 6 Using Technology to Make It Easy   141

26. Upgrade Office Efficiency with Computers,
    Laptops, and Networks   145

27. Make Use of Cell Phones, Pagers, Wireless
Handhelds, and Other Handheld Devices 150

28. Understand the Differences between DSL, Cable
Modems, ISDN, and T-1 Lines 153

29. Make Teleconferencing and Videoconferencing
Work for You 156

30. Use Software to Help Solve Everyday Problems 160

31. Learn How to Design and Update Your Company's
Web Site 163

32. Continue Your Computer Education 168

Top Tips for Saving Money When Buying Technology 170

CHAPTER 7 Managing Stress 173

33. Take Frequent Breaks 178

34. Exercise at Your Desk, during Breaks, or at Lunch 180

35. Watch What You Eat 184

36. Consider Office Yoga, Feng Shui, Meditation,
and Massage 187

37. Create Nap Rooms and Nursing Spaces for
Working Moms 191

38. Look into Flextime and Comp Time 194

Top Tips for Relieving Stress at the Office 196

Acknowledgments 199

Index 201

About the Author 210

Letter from Quill's President

Welcome to *The* Really *Useful Guide to Working Smarter, Not Harder.* This book is the result of Quill's desire to find something we could share with our customers that will bring real value to them every day on the job. Quill is all about making life as easy as possible for our customers. We constantly strive to do that through our products, services, and low prices. So what else could we do for our customers that demonstrates our commitment and support? We decided to develop a book that will give you some true, practical information.

Every year, Quill holds focus groups around the country with customers and noncustomers alike. We want to learn first-hand what issues and challenges people face on their jobs, how they feel about office products in general, and what else Quill can do to make their jobs easier. Over the last few years, one theme has come through very clearly—everyone is pressed for time. It is the thing that none of us ever has enough of. I remember one woman in suburban Chicago saying how thrilled she was with Quill's online ordering because she could order supplies and still keep talking on the phone to carry out some other part of her duties. Regardless of our job title or responsibilities, we are all pressed for time. So Quill made it a priority to address that issue with this exclusive how-to book.

We teamed up with Ilyce Glink, a very well-known author who has written many other books designed to help people with various aspects of their lives. You may have even seen Ilyce on television. She is a regular contributor to WGN-TV Chicago, the nation's Superstation. She's also appeared on other shows, including *Oprah* and the *Today Show,* to discuss ways people can improve and simplify their lives. Ilyce and her staff spent several weeks interviewing hundreds of Quill customers to get a clearer picture of how people felt about their jobs and the time pressures they faced. In this book, you will find that we've addressed many of the topics that you, the Quill customers, identified. Many of the recommendations came directly from you. Subjects like time management, organization, ergonomics, relationship building, and many more are dealt with in a very easy-to-read and extremely helpful manner.

I hope you will enjoy the book and keep it as a reference guide for your workplace. We know how busy you are and how much people in your organization depend on you. The typical Quill customer usually wears many hats—I have even heard people describe their function as "chief cook and bottle washer." We can all relate to that. We want you to know you can always depend on Quill. No matter how busy things get, we are always here to help.

Happy reading.

Larry Morse
President, Quill Corporation
March 2003

P.S. I would love to hear what you think of this book. You can reach me at larry.morse@quill.com with your comments.

Introduction

Wouldn't it be wonderful to find an extra few hours in the day? If you could squeeze even thirty extra minutes into your workday, every day, you'd finally have *nearly* enough time to get everything done that's been heaped upon your plate.

Of course, you could always work late in order to keep up—and many of you reading this book are nodding, "I already *do* work late!" Working late is okay once in a while, but it's not a long-term answer.

And, unfortunately, despite copious amounts of research, I was unable to come up with a single spell that would magically add time to an eight-hour day.

The good news is that you have the answer right in front of you. *The* Really *Useful Guide to Working Smarter, Not Harder* shows you easy ways to make the most of your time on the job. When you work smarter, you're better able to organize your time. You're up to date on which technologies can keep you on track. You know where to go to find the information you need quickly.

But this book goes beyond the basics to help you tone down your stress level at work while tuning up your office environment. It offers tips on delegating assignments and improving your relationships with your colleagues and bosses. I've even included some ways you can nicely say no—and preserve your sanity.

Today, most offices operate at a pace that can only be described as frenzied, as we all try to make the most of what we have in a difficult economic time. *The* Really *Useful Guide to Working Smarter, Not Harder* gives you the tips and information you need to not only get everything done, but do it with style.

Let's get going.

CHAPTER 1

Managing Your Time

Making the Most of the Hours You Work

Once she got promoted, Diedra just couldn't seem to get it all done in eight hours. She would start projects and finish them late, if at all. Her colleagues helped keep her on schedule for a while, but eventually their own work had to come first. Diedra's boss sat her down and asked her what was happening. Diedra finally admitted that she was in over her head. She knew how to do the new assignments, but she just couldn't manage her time well enough to make it all happen.

Managing your time well means making the most of each hour you work. You have to think about when you do your best work during the day, what makes you the most (or least) productive, and how you can get moving faster without sacrificing quality.

With some time-management guidance from her boss, Diedra eventually grew into her new job and figured out what she needed to do to get everything done. But everyone isn't lucky enough to get that kind of guidance. So it's up to us to figure it out for ourselves.

Making the most of the hours you work could mean shifting your hours to better suit your natural body clock (for example, starting and ending earlier), or it could mean working through lunch while eating at your desk. Most likely, you'll have to take a close look at how you manage each hour and identify the ways in which you're wasting time.

This chapter offers specific strategies for tracking your time and finding ways to make an hour feel like two. It should help you define which projects are most important (and which can be left until later).

1 Really Useful Tip

Don't Mistake a Fire for an Inferno

It always seems like something comes up right when you're really rolling on a project. Typically, it's something marked "URGENT," though whether it is urgent to you (certainly it is urgent to the person who sent the project your way) may be open to debate.

How you deal with urgent matters that come to your attention says a lot about your time-management skills. While dropping everything to tackle the problem may be the first solution that comes to your mind, it may not be the best use of your time.

Clearly, fires have to be contained and put out. But small fires are not so urgent as infernos, and mistaking a small fire for an inferno can cost you in lost time and productivity.

How can you tell what's *really* important? If it will affect either the immediate quality of the product or service you provide or the relationship you have with a customer, it's a drop-everything kind of problem. These kinds of problems feel like infernos because you usually have to take several layers of action all at once. Everyone works flat out, pitching in, to get the situation straightened out.

Most other "fires" are the result of someone else's lack of planning. As my Uncle Rich likes to say, "Lack of planning on your part does not constitute an emergency on my part."

If there's one coworker or colleague who depends on you frequently to help him or her put out fires or infernos, you have to learn how to say no—and mean it. It's a mistake for this individual to depend on you to pull the project out of the hat at the last moment. Saying no will help you find extra time for your own work, and it will force your colleague to rely on him- or herself instead of on you. (For some ways to say no nicely, see page 19.)

If you find yourself getting sucked into putting out fires and infernos on a regular basis, start keeping a "Fires and Infernos" log. After every fire or inferno, make an entry in your log, noting how long it took to put it out.

After a week or two of keeping the log, go back over it and ask yourself, "How could I have avoided this situation, and how can I avoid it in the future?" Pay special attention to how much time you spent putting out fires and infernos, and mentally calculate how that lost time could be put to better use in your workday. This will be that extra motivation you may need to help you handle both fires and infernos more efficiently. Once you have determined how to avoid these urgent and not-so-urgent problems, you'll be able to sidestep them the next time.

And once you're able to distinguish the fires from the infernos, you'll be more efficient as well. Quick identification of the problem will save you time, especially if it's a fire masquerading as an inferno.

2 Really Useful Tip

Avoid the Seven Deadly Time Traps

Have you ever noticed how some projects just seem to take forever? It could be a phone call that gets away from you, or an important assignment that seems to soak up all the available energy you have in an afternoon.

Time traps literally eat up precious minutes and hours of your day, delaying other important things on your to-do list. Here are some of the most common time traps and how you can avoid them:

1. Meeting Mayhem

You or your boss gets called into a meeting that stretches on forever. Or you have a day's worth of meetings scheduled back-to-back. Or your morning meeting is simply a rundown of information you've already read—in other words, a complete waste of time.

If you don't know when the meeting is supposed to start and end, and if you don't have a firm agenda, then this is a meeting that will probably waste everyone's time.

Caleigh has meetings like this almost every week. She works for a large school district on the East coast and complains that about 75 percent of her meetings are completely useless. When she gets out of a meeting, she feels "draggy" and "tired," and it takes her a while to ramp up again. Some weeks, the meetings are so onerous that she has to work late—and overtime makes her boss cranky.

"If I could just get out of some of these meetings, or at least spend *less* time there, I know I could be more productive and get everything else done," she said.

Avoiding the time trap: If you're running a meeting or setting one up for your boss, aim to keep it as short as possible. Ask yourself: Is this meeting really necessary? If the answer is no or maybe, try to distribute the information rather than calling a meeting to discuss it.

If you have to call a meeting, write a detailed agenda that gives everyone a little background on the topics that are going to be discussed. A few sentences will give the group a starting point for discussion. E-mail the agenda before the meeting so everyone knows what's going on. Once you're in the meeting, don't waste time reading the agenda or any handouts. Typically, people attending the meeting will either know this information already or can scan it quickly as the meeting begins.

When learning the craft, screenwriters are often taught to start a scene in the middle and get out before it's over. In other words, grab the audience's attention by getting to the heart of the matter as quickly as possible. When you're running a meeting, you want to do the same. Skip the back story and get to the issue at hand right away. You'll energize your team and shave precious minutes off your meeting time.

Finally, set a start and end time for each meeting—then stick to it. When I was president of a nonprofit journalism organization, I started and ended my meetings promptly. I also held them at the same time each month. If you showed up five minutes late, you quickly figured out that we hadn't waited for you.

After a few months, everyone realized that our meetings started and ended promptly and that as a result no one was ever late for work. These focused, quick meetings gave everyone an energetic start to the day. And because they weren't seen as a waste of time, board members started coming to all of the meetings. (As an added incentive, I brought donuts and bagels—the ubiquitous "spoonful of sugar" never hurts!)

2. Colleagues Who Like to Chitchat

Sometimes I think watercoolers (and copiers, break rooms, and other places office workers congregate) should be banned. Just think about how much more time we'd have in a day!

Seriously, breaks are good for the mind and soul—and it's important to stay hydrated—but it's way too easy to get caught up in a lengthy conversation about the weekend, dating, family life, restaurants, sports scores . . . and before you know it, another fifteen minutes is down the drain. If you don't have anything else to do, then chitchat is a terrific time filler. But if you're wasting too much time, you need to get your chatty colleagues under control.

Avoiding the time trap: One way to cut down on chitchat is to avoid your colleagues. But that's easier said than done. When you work in an open cubicle, or in an office without walls, people are around you all the time. You hear them talk to one another, unintentionally eavesdrop on their phone calls, and watch them walk around. It's natural to be distracted, especially if you have an unpleasant project on your desk at the time.

Avoiding the watercooler isn't that difficult. Just bring a water bottle from home, fill it up in the morning, and sip it during the day.

What should you do if someone drops by your desk and you don't have time to talk? Mary, a village clerk, stands up. She says that when she stands up, the other person gets the message that he has overstayed his welcome and moves on.

Another helpful trick is to always have a stack of papers, briefcase, pile of books, or other onerous-looking work-related stuff around. That way, you can say, "I'd love to chat, but I've got a mound of work. Want to have lunch?"

Be prepared with a few excuses: "No time to chat today, I've got to get out of here right at 5:00 P.M." is something that almost everyone understands.

3. Customers or Colleagues Who Need Hand-Holding

When a customer calls, your first instinct should be to do anything and everything you can to make her or keep her happy. Research shows that customers who feel they can depend on you will stay loyal to your product or brand. And if you're the contact person for consumers (at the other end of a toll-free number), you'll need to be polite.

But that doesn't mean you have to let yourself be dragged into long conversations. Listening to the problem and finding a solution are important, but getting dumped on or being forced to fill the role of psychiatrist is quite another matter.

If you have to hand-hold a customer, at least you can justify it by saying that it's good for the company. But unless you're in a mentoring relationship, hand-holding a needy colleague can quickly become a time trap. That's a situation you'll want to avoid.

Avoiding the time trap: When a customer calls, try to get him or her to identify the issue at hand as quickly as possible. Ask him, "How can I *help* you today?" If you continue to repeat the question every time the caller veers off in another direction, you'll be able to focus him. If there is no ready solution, keep a message pad handy so you can record the customer's number, information, and question or complaint. Reassure the caller that someone will get back to him soon. Aim to keep these calls to less than five minutes.

If the time trap involves a colleague who needs hand-holding, you should try to keep him or her as focused as possible. If the problem can't be resolved in a few minutes, schedule a lunch date or prework breakfast to talk more about it.

4. Messy Desks and Disorganized Files

My father used to have a T-shirt that said, "A clean desk is the sign of a sick mind." Perhaps it is. I know many highly intelligent, creative people who have disorganized offices (not to mention lives).

Ellen has a big job with the State of Illinois. But you should see the state of her office: large stacks of briefings, notes, papers, unread newspapers, and to-do lists have accumulated like stalagmites in a cave. There is so much stuff piled everywhere that it's difficult for her to reach her keyboard and telephone! And yet, she claims that she knows where everything is at all times—it just takes her a while to locate it.

The problem with clutter is that it takes so much time to find anything. Even if you think you know where something is, precious minutes slip away as you try to locate it. Worse yet, if someone else needs to find something in your office, it's unlikely he or she will be able sift through your stacks as quickly as you would be able to.

Having a clean desk and organized files also saves time on a daily basis—once all of the cleaning and organizing has been done.

Avoiding the time trap: Some people (and I include myself in this category) find it difficult to keep things organized. But though I fought it for many years, even I have to admit that it's a whole lot easier to find something when it's put away in the right place.

Deborah, a producer for a television show, saw firsthand how organization could work for her. She had a cubicle that was piled high with tapes, press releases, CDs, newspapers, books, and other materials that publicists send when trying to get their products and people on TV. One day, an organizational expert came on the show and used Deborah's desk as an example of how a little organization can make a huge difference in productivity. Deborah has kept her desk clean and organized ever since and can't believe how much less time it takes to maintain her newly organized work life.

Chapter 2 of this book is filled with easy ways you can organize your desk and your life. What's worked for me? The basics: plastic drawers on wheels, colored hanging file folders, and a label maker.

5. Interruptions

There are two kinds of interruptions that can eat into your workday: those you can't stop and those you can. Either way, they can be frustrating and time-consuming, not only because you have to stop what you're working on to deal with whatever has interrupted you, but also because once you've dealt with it, it will take a few minutes to get back into your former mind-set.

Avoiding the time trap: A little planning can go a long way toward making sure that interruptions are kept to a minimum. If you know ahead of time when a big project is going to land on your desk, you can easily set aside time for it first thing in the morning, when colleagues are busy working on their own projects. Once you have the big projects of the day finished, you'll just have those smaller projects, and refocusing after an interruption will be easier.

If your interruptions are phone based, see if you and another colleague can take turns answering the phone. For example, from 10:00 A.M. to noon, you cover her phone, and from 1:00 P.M. to 3:00 P.M., she covers your phone. That will give you larger blocks of uninterrupted time to make sure that everything gets done.

You might also want to learn to say no and later (but in a nice way, of course), when appropriate. There are coworkers who will quickly learn to take advantage of your good nature if you always agree to take on extra work. By saying no, you'll keep those interruptions to a minimum.

6. Procrastination

Putting off something until tomorrow won't make it go away. Delaying the inevitable just makes the task or project seem a whole lot bigger and more difficult than it really is. If you procrastinate long enough, you can work yourself into a stubborn mind-set that makes it impossible to accomplish anything.

Procrastination is a psychological game we play with ourselves. Even though we know intellectually that we have to get certain tasks accomplished in a specific time frame, some of us have a harder time getting motivated. So we think, *I still have enough time to get this project done. I don't have to do this now.* What ends up happening to most procrastinators is that we wait until the last moment—and then we rush the job.

Journalists tend to be great procrastinators. They get an adrenaline rush from waiting until the last possible moment to write a story, then filtering the information through their brains and, well, "cranking it out."

But is the story you've written, or the project you've just completed, any better because you've waited until the last moment? Probably not. You leave yourself no time whatsoever to check your work and make sure it's the best job you could have done.

Avoiding the time trap: If procrastination is a mind game, then to beat it you'll have to play along.

Make a list of everything you have to do. Then, reorganize the list. Put your least-favorite tasks at the top and your favorite tasks at the bottom. Every day, make sure you do your least-favorite tasks first, right when you start your shift.

By attacking your least-favorite projects first, when you have the most mental energy, you'll do them in half the time, and beat your deadlines. Plus, you'll look forward to the rest of your day.

7. Overscheduling and Multitasking

If your work life operates on a packed schedule, you're probably not getting much of your real work done. You're too busy shuttling between appointments and meetings and searching for stuff on top of or next to your desk.

And multitasking isn't the answer. New research shows that doing several things simultaneously can be a huge time waster. The University of Michigan revealed this with a study that looked at how people attacked math problems. Study participants who divided their time between two sets of math problems took 50 percent longer to complete them than those participants who tackled one set of problems at a time.

That's because any time you switch between two or three different tasks, there's a start-up cost, according to Dr. Joshua Rubinstein, one of the study's authors. And you're more likely to make mistakes. (For more details on the study, see page 26.)

If you think about it, the concept of every project having a start-up cost is true. While I was writing this section of the book, I got a call from another reporter who wanted to interview me for a story on things everyone can do in sixty minutes that will have a positive impact on his or her finances. It took us a couple of minutes to get into the conversation, and after it was over, I found I couldn't immediately get started on my next thought for the book.

Instead, I got up, walked to the front door, walked outside to see what was going on with the house that's being built two doors down, checked for the mail (which hadn't arrived), came back inside, stretched, walked back to the kitchen counter where I had been working, and sat down. Time lost? About five minutes.

Imagine switching back and forth between projects all day long. You could easily lose an hour or more. What a time trap!

Avoiding the time trap: If you're losing time by having to switch between projects frequently, you've got to reorganize your day so that you have time to tackle all the things on your to-do list.

If your office life operates on schedules, be sure to schedule in an hour or two each day to work on specific tasks that need your complete attention. If you need to order supplies, get payables signed, or take care of your boss's expenses from a recent trip, schedule it into your day so that it doesn't fall by the wayside.

Another idea is to simply batch together similar projects. If you shut off your phone for an hour to focus on a group of similar tasks, you'll move through them quickly. If you then pick up your messages and return calls, you'll do that more quickly too.

Finally, you may want to reorganize your day to suit your personal energy levels. Studies show that most people work faster in the morning and slow down after lunch, with productivity dropping off the edge of the cliff about eight to ten hours after people wake up.

If you're working twice as fast in the morning as you are in the late afternoon, approach your boss about starting your shift a half-hour earlier. It could save you a full hour in the long run.

Finding the Time Traps in Your Day

How do you find the time traps in your day? The easiest suggestion is to take a page from dieters and money managers, who record, respectively, every morsel of food they consume and every penny they spend.

Keep a daily log of each project you finish, how long the project took to finish, and what time of day you finished it. When I do this, I use a small spiral-bound notepad that I can easily slip into my purse or pocket.

If you spend fifteen minutes on mailing letters, record that. If you spend five minutes on a telephone call, record that. Although keeping your log will be time-consuming at first, it will soon show you where you get bogged down and what projects tend to be the biggest time traps in your day.

You'll also want to record how many breaks you take each day. These breaks could be physical—getting up from your seat—or mental, including daydreaming and rescheduling breaks.

Note your meetings, but also keep track of "drop-by" meetings, whether for business or to chat. How long do your colleagues keep you away from your work each day? You could easily be wasting an hour a day and never know it.

Time priorities. Once you've kept your log for a week or two, analyze the results. Take a bunch of different colored highlighters. Highlight all of your scheduled meetings in one color, your impromptu meetings with colleagues in another color. Put your phone calls in a third color, and assign different colors to your other tasks. Tally up all the colors and see where you're spending most of your time and how much time you're wasting in a day on chitchat.

The whole goal of the exercise is to figure out how to make your day move easier, faster, and more productively. Focus on that and you'll soon be able to spot the time traps in your workday.

Handheld computers, also known as PDAs, have become all the rage as their price point has dropped. These palm-sized computers are your address book and your calendar. By carrying one with you, you'll always know what's going on, at work and at home.

Bonus Tip

If you have several calendars (one for the office, one for home, one for your kids, one on the kitchen wall), you might find that it's difficult to keep them all up to date. You may frequently double- or triple-schedule yourself simply because it's hard to keep everything updated. (Another time trap, by the way.)

Consider combining your home and work calendars in an electronic format so that instead of updating each individual calendar, you can simply print out an updated weekly or monthly schedule and post it at different locations.

3 Really Useful Tip

Learn How to Prioritize When Everyone's Job Is Hot

When you're working for multiple bosses, life can feel like a high-level political summit—you've got to keep everyone feeling like his or her job is most important.

That's no small task, and the skills you need to keep everyone happy are usually learned at the school of hard knocks. And no matter how you slice it, you're always pitting one boss's work against another's.

Members of the secretarial pool at a major Chicago law firm told me that they would often tell a boss that a particular task would take twice as long as they knew it would so that they'd have enough time to finish something for the other attorneys they worked for.

"We also told them to batch small stuff together. It's easier and faster to work on a half-dozen letters at the same time, then move from letters to briefs to memos," one secretary, Kathy, said.

Another way to get all the jobs done is to simply avoid all interruptions: turn off the phones, log off of e-mail, and shut the door to prevent drop-ins.

Kelly, an administrative assistant in Atlanta, said she has learned how to focus hard and shut out the outside world even though she works in a cubicle next to three other coworkers. "When I'm really concentrating, I don't even hear anyone else," she added.

Judith, an office manager, said that when she really needs to get things done, she wears her telephone headset. "People stay away because they think you're on the phone."

How do you prioritize when everyone's job is hot? Carefully. The administrative assistants I've talked to offer the following suggestions:

Prioritize by job title. If you're doing work for a partner and a senior partner, do the senior partner's work first. Likewise, if you're doing work for a vice president and a manager, complete the work of the person who carries the highest rank in the company. That way, you're protecting yourself.

Prioritize by job importance. If you're working for two bosses of equal stature in the company and both have hot jobs at the same time, complete the task that you think is most important. Often, everyone says that his or her job is hot or most important, but it really isn't. When you first start working at a company, figuring out what's really important is tough. But if you keep your ears and eyes open and pay attention to the work that circulates through your office, you'll quickly learn which projects are truly hot and which are just made to look that way.

Prioritize by pace. When you have two projects that are both important, consider first tackling the project that will require the least amount of time. That way, you'll get to the second project much more quickly.

No matter which way you choose to prioritize, the most important thing you can learn is how to keep everyone feeling like you've made his or her work your priority.

4 Really Useful Tip

Keep on Schedule by Saying No or Later— in a Nice Way

Etiquette and graciousness are powerful tools when you find yourself in a tight spot.

If you're trying to stay on schedule and get everyone's job completed within a reasonable amount of time, it's easy to become frustrated when even more demands are placed upon you.

At the point when your frustration bubbles over, you'll either open your mouth and yell or you'll bottle it all up inside. Wouldn't it be smarter to find a way to diffuse the situation before it becomes too much to bear? Of course it would.

Being nice to everyone is a painless way of buying yourself the freedom to keep on schedule. That's because it allows you to say no and later in a way that won't cause a brouhaha.

Learning how to say things in the right way is the first rule of office politics. Brushing off someone abruptly can quickly label you as rude or unkind. If you say you're going to do something even though you know you'll never get to it, it could damage your reputation as a team player. While saying no can be awkward at times, it's better than saying yes in order to get rid of someone—and then having to face his or her frustration when you haven't done what you said you'd do.

Here are a few nice ways of saying no:

> "I'd like to help out, but I'm swamped right now."
> "I'd like to assist you, but your deadline is a little tight for me."
> "That isn't really my area of expertise. Perhaps Paula (or someone else) could help."

If you have a problem with saying no to requests, practice. I know it sounds silly, but you can practice by sitting down with a close friend, your spouse, or your partner and having that person ask you to do things. Even if you want to do them (I'd love to do some of the projects I'm asked to do), say no. Learn how to say it firmly and not waver. Once you sound like you're intrigued by the project or are giving in slightly, someone can take advantage of you.

And that's what this all comes down to, isn't it? It's about not allowing yourself to be taken advantage of on a regular basis. There's no harm in helping someone out—unless it's going to cause you to miss your own deadlines. If you practice saying no in a nice way, you'll be able to stick to your schedule and maintain your working relationships.

Bonus Tip   If you want a straightforward way of informing your colleagues that you can't help out with every project, try posting a sign with your availability on it. One option would be a dry-erase board that lists the time when you will be available to assist others; for example, "Today I will be available at 2:00 P.M." You can change it to suit your particular schedule. You might also change your voice-mail greeting to say, "Hello, it's Wednesday, October 28, and if you need to reach me, the best time is after 3:00 P.M." That way, you avoid having to explain to everyone who calls why you couldn't call him or her back sooner or were unavailable.

5 Really Useful Tip

Create Schedules, Set Goals, and Keep Everyone Focused

There are three basic types of work that we do from nine to five, or whenever your shift starts and ends:

Busywork. This type of work keeps us active and moving at a fairly fast pace but usually doesn't involve too many brain cells. Examples of busywork might include sorting mail, sending letters, organizing your office, arranging for deliveries, planning an office party, ordering supplies, or returning phone calls.

Small to medium-sized projects. The next level of work might include drafting memos, typing proposals, coordinating documents, tackling an expense report, or even reviewing someone else's work. Administrative assistants say they coordinate several projects of this size each week.

Major projects. In this type of work, you might be coordinating a six-month project, reviewing ordering procedures, or overseeing the implementation of a new filing or computer system.

The bigger the project, the more daunting it seems and the easier it is to procrastinate. The good news is that all projects, big or small, can be broken down into a series of smaller (or, in some cases, much smaller) steps. And by breaking down each step into something on the level of busywork, you'll not only be able to make real progress, but you'll keep the project organized as well.

Here are a few suggestions that can help you keep your project flowing smoothly from start to finish:

Start your planning at the finish line. You need to identify the end goal first if you're going to have any success at all in planning and completing your project. Is the end goal a report? A memo? The installation of a new system at your office? Once you've identified the goal, you can work backward to figure out what steps you have to take to get to it. The last item on the list should be where you start.

Plan out phone calls and meetings in advance. You don't want to waste your time or anyone else's, so make sure you know what you want to accomplish during each phone call or meeting. According to one study, a planned phone call can take seven minutes. An unplanned phone call can take twelve minutes. It will only take you a minute or two to plan each call, which means you could save three minutes on each call. While that doesn't sound like much in the short term, saving three minutes on each call adds up to an hour saved for every 20 phone calls, and a day saved for every 160 calls—easily what you'd make over the course of a major project.

Spend time organizing your project filing system before you start the project. It's a good idea to have a separate filing system for each project you work on.

For example, when I start writing a book, I dedicate one or two plastic filing tubs to the project and fill them with hanging files (personally, I like the brightly colored ones). Each chapter of the book gets it's own hanging file or two (depending on how much research goes into each chapter), and each step or tip gets its own manila file folder. As the research grows, the tubs fill up. But because my system is flexible, I can move tips from chapter to chapter and simply relabel the individual file folders. When the book is completed, the tubs get labeled and placed into long-term storage (also known as my basement).

Do your most difficult tasks when you're the freshest.
Everyone has a high-energy point and a low-energy point of their day. I'm a morning person—in fact, a very-early-morning person. I tend to do my clearest and best thinking around 5:00 A.M. It sounds funny, but I find that if I get up that early, I can get more done from 5:00 A.M. to 7:00 A.M. than I can if I work from 9:00 A.M. to 2:00 P.M.

To be the most productive at your job, it helps to do your most difficult tasks when you have the most mental energy. When it comes to long-term projects, take a few minutes at the end of the day to plan out when you're going to tackle the next aspects of the job. Make sure you schedule your more difficult tasks for when you're the most energetic—typically at the beginning of your shift.

Software can help. There are excellent project-management programs that can help you schedule complicated long-term projects. If you're working with several people or overseeing several people's work, these programs can help you stay informed of which tasks have been completed and where people are on their other assignments. One of the better, and easier to use, programs is Microsoft Scheduler.

Think through the timeline before you say yes. Sometimes you're told when a project has to be finished, and you have no choice but to work within that time frame. However, if your boss asks you how long it will take to complete a project, make sure you carefully think through the timetable before you commit to an end date.

You may even want to build in some additional time in case something comes up that you haven't planned on. With home construction or renovation projects, contractors will typically build in extra time just to cover any contingency. You should consider doing the same with a complex project. It's a win-win situation for you, because if you complete the project early you're a hero, and if you're running late you've already built in the extra time you need.

Spend time communicating with your project mates. Office workers often complain that they're left out of the "information loop." If you want your coworkers to cooperate with you and make your project an important part of their day, you need to communicate with them frequently to make them feel like they're part of your team.

Consider updating the team weekly to let them know where you are on the project and how everyone is doing. You can create a 100-percent bar to track the progress you're making each week. If there are changes to the schedule or project, don't just mention them once to the team member they affect. Instead, make sure you reiterate the change and update everyone in a weekly e-mail. Just remember to keep it short and sweet.

6 Really Useful Tip

Don't Rely on Multitasking to Make You More Productive

Why does one bank pull in twice as many deposits as its competitor down the street? Why does a modern steel plant make steel in thirty minutes while a hundred-year-old plant takes eleven hours? Why are the most productive companies in the world so, well, productive?

Jason Jennings, a best-selling author, consultant, and lecturer, studied why some companies seem to have found the key to productivity while others are stuck in the mud. Why, for example, does the average furniture store sell four thousand dollars' worth of furniture per employee while IKEA sells a hundred thousand dollars' worth per employee?

Jennings, who at age twenty-two became the youngest radio station owner in history, used to believe technology drove productivity. And that's how he went into the research phase of his book *Less Is More.* Instead, he found that having a system that flows beats technology any day of the week.

Think of a well-oiled machine that does its job over and over again. Or, for a real-world example, think about how Southwest Airlines gets most of its airplanes into the terminal and ready to leave again in twenty minutes.

"While writing the book, I hung out with CEOs, workers, vendors, and suppliers. I have been very successful in business and thought I knew a lot about business. But every day I was humbled. Everything that everyone believes about productivity is wrong," Jennings said.

While productivity has soared in the past decade, it's not necessarily a result of multitasking—doing several things at the same time.

In fact, argues Dr. David Meyer, who with Dr. Joshua Rubinstein and Dr. Jeffrey Evans wrote an article called "Executive Control of Cognitive Processes in Task Switching," multitasking is based on a post-layoff corporate assumption that if two people leave, the remaining worker can do the work of three.

What's an example of the worst kind of multitasking? Driving while talking on a cell phone. Even a hands-free, voice-activated cell phone can distract you momentarily—long enough to possibly cause an accident.

"We found the switch cost increases with the complexity of the task," Rubinstein told CNN. "That suggests that a very simple conversation on the phone while driving a car—maybe 'Honey, please pick up some bread on the way home'—might not draw too much concentration. But if the conversation becomes difficult or emotionally charged or mentally taxing—like 'Honey, the house is burning down. What should I do?'—it draws more attention and more mental resources away from your primary task, which is driving the car."

Other kinds of multitasking—like making business calls while running to a meeting—cost you time and can cause you to make a critical mistake. Another example is trying to get work done for two bosses at exactly the same moment. Or talking on the phone while sending an e-mail.

What can you do?

Time the switch. When you find yourself doing several things at the same time, switching back and forth between them, take note of how long it takes you to get back up to speed once

You can keep track of your time with something as simple as a steno pad (use a different page for each day) or with a more complicated calendar that already has the hours printed on it.

you've switched to a new project. That's the time cost of switching. The Meyer/Rubinstein/Evans study found that a switch can cost you ten minutes. Once you're aware of how much time you're losing, you'll be more motivated to try other ways to improve productivity.

Slow it down. Concentrate on getting each job done correctly and as quickly as possible. Rushing to finish all the jobs you're working on will almost certainly result in mistakes.

Avoid time traps. Use some of the tools we talked about earlier in the book, such as keeping a daily log (to find the places where time slips away in your day) and stacking things on your visitor's chair and in your inbox (to keep people and their personal and professional disasters from backing up your workflow).

Save multitasking for the easy stuff. Remember that multitasking works best when you are trying to accomplish tasks that aren't particularly complicated, such as answering the phone while you're surfing the Internet for information.

7 Really Useful Tip

Learn How to Know When You've Done Enough

Time-management experts say that striving for perfection is a bad thing. Fred Kiesner, Hilton chair of entrepreneurship at Loyola Marymount University in Los Angeles, goes so far as to say, "Perfectionism is your enemy."

"So many people don't turn in work. They never get things done. They never start a business because they're waiting until it's perfect. Life isn't perfect—you're always doing things that are less than optimal," Kiesner said.

So when do you turn off the spigot?

Sally, an administrative assistant in Oregon, says she uses the clock. "When the day ends, I plan out the next day, turn off the lights, and go home. I find that it keeps me from obsessing about all of the different things that went wrong that day, things I could have done better."

Robert, an account executive with an advertising firm, says he allows himself to feel bad for a few minutes if something doesn't work or if his boss absolutely hates a new campaign he's created, but then he moves on.

"It's too easy to start worrying about every detail. If I'm concerned about whether someone is going to love or hate the next thing I do, it will limit my creativity, which will kill my ability to do my job," he noted.

The truth is, there are no perfect meetings, no perfect work assignments, no perfect bosses, and no perfect jobs. People create their own hurdles, their own obstacles, their own reasons for not getting the job done. In some ways, experts say, perfectionism is a mind game some of us play in order not to have to do our jobs.

If you are a person who tends toward perfectionism, set boundaries for yourself. Say you won't work past five o'clock, you'll never miss a deadline (even if the project isn't exactly where you want it to be), or you'll do better next time. As humans, we're improving ourselves all the time. If you were to achieve perfection, what challenges would be left in life?

TOP TIPS
for Managing Your Time

*"People don't plan to fail, but
a lot of people do fail to plan."*

Time is precious, and the eight (or ten) hours we spend at work each day typically aren't enough to get everything done. Here are a few ways to make better use of your day:

Plan your day the night before. After you've wound down from the day, take a minute or two to look over your schedule for the next day and the rest of the week. Make sure tomorrow's list of things to do contains everything that *has* to get done.

Overschedule a little. Busy people tend to be more productive. (I know I'm more productive when I have a busy day with a million things on my to-do list.) If you pack your schedule with a few extra items, you might just surprise yourself and get them accomplished.

Prioritize. Organize your day so that you do your most difficult or important tasks first, when you've got the most mental energy.

Work with your energy flow. Some people are morning people, and some, like my assistant, Jennifer, could work through the night and never think twice about it. If you're more awake after lunch, then make sure your afternoon is packed with the important stuff.

Align your time with when you're needed. If your boss comes in at 7:00 A.M. and works twelve hours straight, you can't be there to help out whenever he or she needs you (unless your firm pays overtime and you don't mind spending those extra hours at the office). But if your boss needs you more from 8:00 to 4:00 than from 9:00 to 5:00, ask if you can adjust your hours to better suit your boss's needs. You might find that you're more productive from 8:00 to 4:00, or from 10:00 to 6:00, than from 9:00 to 5:00.

Don't cry over spilt milk. If an assignment doesn't work out, or if you have to redo something, get over it and move on. Time-management experts say a drawn-out mourning period only serves to squelch your productivity, leaving you with more work to do and less time to get it done.

Schedule smart meetings. Try to schedule twenty- to thirty-minute meetings that back up onto something important—like lunch or the end of the day. Time-management experts say the rumbling of stomachs and our desire to get home at the end of the day are powerful motivators.

Stay organized. If you don't know where things are, you'll waste minutes or hours each day trying to find them—which adds up to lost days over the course of a year. Several times a week, make organizing your workspace the last thing you do before you shut off the lights. (For more tips on staying organized, see chapter 2.)

CHAPTER 2

Organizing Your Office

Why Organizing Your Office Can Energize Your Day

I recently walked into a messy house. I mean a house with four kids, a dog, and every single Lego brick ever made strewn about the floor. You had to be careful or you'd step on something. The kids and the dog didn't seem to mind, but the mother seemed a bit distracted.

That's what clutter and disorganization do to us—they distract us from whatever it is we need to do during the day. We end up wading through the mess, trying to find documents we need, phone numbers we scribbled on a pad somewhere, disks with important files, receipts for business expenses, and so on.

Some people find it really difficult to keep things neat and clean. Others are just naturally good at it.

My friend Emanuele is a natural organizer. When she bought her current residence, her husband was on a business trip. Inside a week or so, she had packed up her whole house, moved to the new place, had it painted, and unpacked just about all of the boxes. No matter what time of day you'd go over to her place, it would be neat, organized, and clean.

There's a positive energy that flows from being organized. The Chinese would call it "chi" and talk about Feng Shui (see page 188 for more details about Feng Shui and how it might work in your office). But I like to think that the energy comes from being focused and productive because you're not distracted by the mess and clutter.

When my office is clean, the desk uncluttered, the files put away, and the books straightened on their shelves, I feel better about where I am and what I have to do during the day. A clean desk means I get to dig in and get started *right now*. I don't have to wait to clear things away or stack them somewhere else until later.

(This doesn't just work in my office. I feel *really* good when I walk into a spotless kitchen at the end of the day!)

Of course, I'm not my friend Emanuele. I'm a little more like my father, Ronald, an attorney who kept all of his files on the floor and stacked around his office but claimed he knew exactly where everything was all the time. But I fight the urge to let clutter accumulate because it feels so much better to get everything up off the floor and put away.

If your office isn't completely clean and organized, take heart. In a few hours it can be.

8 Really Useful Tip

Create a Filing System That Works for You

The smartest thing I've ever heard anyone say about filing is that it isn't about storing documents—it's about retrieving them.

When you create a filing system, you're probably thinking about keeping things organized. But what you should really be thinking about is how to create a filing system that makes it easier for you (or anyone else) to find something when it's needed.

Too often, people get caught up in the storage part of the equation—more specifically, they start to think that everything needs to be saved because they're sure it'll be needed the minute *after* it gets tossed. (I'm guilty of this myself!) So the decision about whether something actually needs to be filed is never made. You assume that because a piece of paper has crossed your desk, it's destined for a file somewhere, somehow.

That's how filing systems end up growing into storage rooms, which then grow into large long-term storage facilities, and finally into deep, deep storage for documents that may never again see the light of day.

Before you can avoid this filing trap, you first have to make a decision about what needs to be kept and what can be tossed.

Keep It or Toss It
According to the Association for Information and Image Management, U.S. businesses are producing more than 2.7

billion sheets of file-folder contents every day. Whenever you handle a document or piece of paper, you have to make a decision about what to do with it. Typically, you will either:

✓ File it

✓ Use it

✓ Toss it

Although it's easier to decide later what to do with a particular piece of paper, it's important to train yourself to make an instant decision. If you don't know what you want to do with something, ask yourself these questions:

✓ Will I need to refer to this item again?

✓ How easy is it to replace this item?

✓ Do I have contact information (name, address, phone number, e-mail) for the person who sent this item in case I need to have them resend it?

✓ Is this document an original, and will I need it as an original in the future?

✓ Can an electronic copy be sent instead or can I scan this and throw it away? (E-copies are easier to store than paper.)

By the way, don't feel bad about tossing something. In today's techno-world, it's easy to get copies of most documents. You can also scan something into your computer and keep an electronic copy of it. (See page 49 for details on creating or updating your electronic filing system.)

Find a Place to Put It

If you've decided to toss something, there's the circular file. If you've decided to either file it or do something with it, you need to put it somewhere until you're ready to take that step. Here are two suggestions:

Julie, a legal secretary, used to allow everyone to throw everything into an inbox, including mail, documents, memos, etc. Her mornings were typically spent sorting through each document to figure out what needed to be done with it.

This "legal triage," as she called it, was eliminated when she created a vertical standing file on top of her desk. The six file folders she created included:

ASAP jobs. This folder, which sits in front, includes any rush jobs or those needing immediate attention.

Current projects. For those items that Julie works on during the day.

Filing. For whenever there's time.

Seminar information. Julie's bosses frequently attend conferences, so in this file she has applications, registrations, airline tickets and reservations, hotel information, and a calendar of annual events that are attended.

Personal. For phone numbers, personal correspondence, forms that need to be filled out for human resources, tax information, etc.

Back burner. This file includes documents Julie looks at when she has time.

You could change what the folders are called, but the idea is to have about half a dozen folders that take care of any immediate contingency. What's really nice about Julie's system is that she trained everyone at work to use it rather than simply dumping everything in the inbox.

"It helps everyone identify what they have and make a decision about how quickly it needs to be dealt with. That saves me time because I don't have to look through it and make my own decision," Julie noted.

In addition to replacing her inbox with a system similar to Julie's, Kathleen, an administrative assistant at a steel company, also uses a date folder for things that have to be done later in the month. (It functions as her tickler file.) Each compartment is labeled with a number to correspond with each day in the month, and she files mail, responses, bills, and other documents by the date they're due. Every day she checks that day for anything urgent that has to go out.

You could call Julie's and Kathleen's systems the first level of filing. You've made the initial decision about whether to toss or keep your document, and you've stored it in an organized place that makes its retrieval a piece of cake.

Once you've completed a project or job, you have to decide whether it deserves to be stored long-term in your filing system or tossed.

What should you keep? Anything that you would have a tough time replacing. In the legal world, that might include evidence for a case or any original documents. In the business world, you might keep proprietary information, such as client files, sales information, and marketing plans. Talk to your boss about what information he or she thinks is important to keep and whether it needs to be immediately accessible or can be put in long-term storage.

Creating Your Files

There are several different types of filing systems you may use in a single office. For example, I have an accordion file folder for each year's business receipts. At the end of the year, I put a rubber band around the file and carry it downstairs to long-term storage.

I also have files for the different types of business that I do. I keep files about my television stories or radio programs organized by date. My book files are organized by subject, as are my two general-subject research files.

The key thing is to figure out which way works best for your documents. Here are some of the most common and easiest ways to file:

Alphabetically. If you're filing by name, category, or topic, this is a good option and allows for quick retrieval.

By subject or project. If you need to create subfolders or subcategories of information, you might go this way.

By date. If you're filing bills, purchase orders, or other time-sensitive documents, filing by date helps. It also helps to organize backup files that are set up by month.

By place. If your company has satellite offices or warehouses, or if your business is divided up regionally, this might work for you.

With tickler files. If you need to be reminded of things to do later in the month, these files are an easy way.

Building Your Filing System

Creating a filing system from scratch takes time. But the materials are pretty basic. Here is a list of all the supplies you'll need:

Container. You'll need someplace to put your files. For working files, you might try a filing cabinet (legal- or letter-sized). If you need to be able to access your files from different locations around your office, consider purchasing a filing cabinet on wheels. But spend some time thinking about how the files are going to be used. For example, if your files are project based and are going to stay in the same place until you move them into long-term storage, you might buy large plastic tubs and simply place them on a shelf and store the files in them. When the project is finished, you can put the cover on the tub and move it into long-term storage.

Hanging file folders. Hanging file folders help you keep things organized and separate. They come in all sorts of colors, which are useful for keeping things organized. Choose different colors for clients, accounting, various projects, satellite operations, or however you divide up your files. Colored hanging file folders not only keep things organized, but they brighten up your office as well. Choose legal- or letter-sized, and don't throw out the tabs that come with the box. You'll need them.

Manila folders. You'll need to put the actual documents into something, and the plain manila folder is it. Choose legal- or letter-sized.

Label maker. There are very few things in life we have to have other than food, clothing, shelter, health, and perhaps a little fun on the weekends. But when I saw how great my friend Lori's files looked when she used a label maker instead of handwriting file names, I was smitten and had to have one. Inexpensive and easy to use, label makers give your files a professional look and make them easier to use.

Putting Your Filing Plan into Action

If you're creating a filing system from scratch, it's relatively easy to build your basic folders and get going. If you have to reorganize current files, be prepared for a huge mess before you get a handle on things. Here's how to get it done:

Map out your new filing system. By having a plan, you'll keep track of your progress in an orderly way.

Move through your files one section at a time. Don't try to reorganize the entire office at once.

Spread the word. There's nothing more frustrating than trying to find a file that's been moved elsewhere. If you let people know what you're doing and even distribute copies of your filing map or plan, you'll win over your colleagues and cut down on office grumbling.

Give progress reports. If the retooling of your office filing system is a huge job that will, unfortunately, inconvenience people, try to give progress reports. Think about how cities let their residents know about ongoing roadwork. Consider setting up a sign that shows a 100-percent bar and move an arrow up the bar as you progress.

A lot of people think filing has to be difficult. It doesn't. It just requires organization. For a few more advanced filing tips, read on.

9 Really Useful Tip

Move Ahead with Advanced Filing Tips

Every once in a while you'll encounter something that doesn't fit neatly into a manila folder—even one that's legal-sized.

If you work for a company that uses samples to sell or demonstrate a product, or if you work for an architectural firm, developer, or mapping company that uses large prints, maps, or aerial photographs, you could end up with plenty of oddly shaped items and nowhere to store them.

Fortunately, today's office-supply designers have come up with solutions to fit almost every need:

Oversized storage containers. Office-supply manufacturers have designed boxes that are bigger and longer than standard storage containers to hold both samples and hanging file folders. It would be easy to use one box or several for a project that includes both. If what you're storing is delicate, you can purchase fillers (polystyrene peanuts, bubble wrap, puff balls, etc.) to keep the object stable while it's in storage.

Cardboard, metal, or plastic holders. These containers can be placed on a bookshelf and are excellent for storing magazines, catalogs, research or conference materials, or other records that need to be stored vertically and are used frequently.

Round or prism-shaped tubes. These accommodate large rolled-up prints, maps, photographs, architectural drawings, and other nonstandard-sized files. They're also useful for shipping these items. Metal standing grids can be used to keep the tubes organized and upright. Use your label maker to create easy-to-read labels so that a map or print doesn't end up in the wrong tube.

Flat files. If you work with drawings, maps, or prints frequently, look into flat filing cabinets. These typically offer ten or fifteen flat drawers that pull straight out, keeping your prints and drawings flat and easily accessible.

Wall files. Think about maximizing space when you're creating your filing system. You want to use every available space in its best way. So if you have a wall (even a cubical wall) that's empty, consider using a wall filing system for your "hot" files, contingency files (ASAP jobs, current filing, seminars, etc.), or even magazines. When a file is hanging on a wall, it's difficult not to see it. (Just make sure your wall is strong enough to handle five hundred to six hundred pieces of paper.)

Three-ring binders. If you need to flip between various documents from time to time (like a year's worth of bank statements), few things work as well as a three-ring binder. It's also flexible enough to allow you to insert or pull out documents easily.

If you haven't seen what you need in someone else's office, peruse an office-supply catalog or search online to get an idea of what's available.

An "out guide" can be used to mark the spot in a file cabinet where you've taken out a file. The nice thing about an out guide is that it helps you quickly find the spot where the file belongs. See Quill.com or a Quill catalog for more information.

Organizing Your Files

Leonora used to use three-cut file folders, which looked neat and organized when she initially set up her filing system. She alternated the folders so that the tabs were set at left, middle, right, left, middle, right, and so on.

But after working with her files for a while, they got messy. If she had to add a folder in the middle, all of the files would get out of order.

The next time she reorganized her files, she bought the same three-tab box but used all of the left tabs for one client, all of the center tabs for a different client, and all of the right tabs for a third client. Each time she needed to add a file, she was able to keep all of the tabs for a client lined up on one side, which made it easy to keep her files neat and organized.

Patricia also discovered the benefits of filing with same-sided tabs and then took it one step further. In addition to color-coding her files (with colored hanging file folders), she also bought three label makers and used different colored labels for different groups of files (clients, financial, internal). She says it helps her keep everything organized.

Heidi uses a different sort of filing technique. As a book editor, her office is littered with dozens of manuscripts in various stages of production. She, and many other editors in the book business, uses bookshelves to keep manuscripts organized and accessible.

Coding and Sorting

In some legal offices, each piece of paper is coded before it is filed. That way, if a document is ever misplaced, all someone has to do is look at the top right-hand corner to know where it should go.

Attorneys, doctors, and other specialists who deal with time-sensitive materials might date- or time-stamp a document before it is filed. Ask your boss if date- or time-stamping is appropriate for your filing system.

Sorting is another useful tool. Most people organize a file with either the oldest or newest document first. Make a decision about what works for you, and then make sure every file is organized the same way. It's confusing to use a filing system in which some files have the oldest document first and others have the newest document first.

Staples, Paper Clips, and Binder Clips

Paper clips gunk up files, as do ripped or crumpled documents. If a document comes to you with paper clips, remove them and staple the pages of the document together. This way, documents won't get stuck to one another.

If a document is ripped, either make a copy of it or repair it. Then staple it, or use binder clips to keep it together.

Throwing Out Old or Older Files

Eventually, most files can be tossed. That doesn't mean you or someone else will actually do the dirty deed—but you could, if you wanted to.

How can you tell if it's time to throw something out? Start by figuring out whether something can go into long-term storage. In most cases, if you haven't had the need for a file in the past three to five years, you can probably put it into long-term storage. Once it's in long-term storage, if you haven't used it in ten years, you can probably toss it for good.

Of course, there are exceptions to this rule. Medical, legal, and business tax records are typically never thrown out. My husband, Sam, continues to store the legal records of almost every single client he has ever assisted. When he was choosing an office space, the place he ended up moving to included an enormous six-hundred-square-foot storage space that was ideal for his long-term files.

There are items you can immediately send to long-term storage. For example, the day I finish writing a book, I transfer all of the research materials to plastic tubs, label them, and send them to long-term storage. Five years after the book is published, I toss the original research files. A few years after a story of mine has run in the newspaper or has aired on the radio, I toss my story and radio program files.

Bonus Tip

The Don'ts of Filing

There are a lot of things you should do when you're filing. But savvy office workers know there are also some things you shouldn't do. Here is my list of filing don'ts:

Don't overstuff your hanging file folders. If you have subfolders that can't sit neatly at the bottom of a hanging folder, start a new hanging folder. Ideally, you won't have more than four manila folders per hanging folder.

Don't overstuff each manila folder. If you have more than three-quarters of an inch of paper in each manila folder, add another folder.

Don't allow your folders to deteriorate. If they start to look worn, faded, or shabby, or if they tear, replace them. Repairing folders with tape and glue is penny-savvy but dollar-foolish. Spend a few extra dollars on new folders so that your filing system continues to work well.

Don't overload your drawers. Overstuffed drawers don't close properly and papers in them could get caught and torn. If you leave a few inches of free room in each drawer, it'll be easier for you to access and retrieve documents.

Don't tab at the back of hanging files. If you create a printed tab and put it at the front of each file, it'll be easier to find what you're looking for.

Don't get lazy about filing. And don't allow your office mates to get lazy either. If replacing documents correctly is a problem in your office, stack used files in a single location and have everyone take turns putting everything back in order at the end of the day. If everyone takes a turn, no one will be as lazy about replacing files.

Don't save multiple copies of the same document. And don't save pamphlets and booklets unless you're really going to need them again and it would be difficult, expensive, or time-consuming to replace them.

On the other hand, I recently spent a day shredding old checks and statements from a checking account I closed back in 1987. (Well, no one's perfect!)

If you're going to throw something out, there are three ways to do it:

Toss it in the circular file. But don't put anything sensitive in here, because people have been known to go through other people's garbage.

Recycle it. Might as well help the environment if you can (and if your company has a "green" program).

Shred it. This is a must for anything that's at all sensitive or personal. If you don't have a shredder, you might want to ask your company to invest in a small one you can keep at your desk.

Make Time for Filing

No matter which filing system you use, schedule an hour a week (or a little more or less time depending on how many documents you generate and process) to keep your filing up to date.

It's helpful to make this your scheduled project before the weekend starts (or before you go on vacation). Coming back on a Monday to an organized desk and filing system allows you to get a jump start on the week's activities.

Bonus Tip

If you're in charge of your office files, you may want to create a file guide. This is a single sheet of paper that tells people where to find things and in what shape you expect the files to be returned. If you are thorough when you write out your file guide, it will become the reference for how your files are kept. Then, when someone new is hired or if a temp comes to fill in, you can give him or her this easy reference guide so your files stay organized.

10 Really Useful Tip

Organize Your Computer Files

According to one study, 95 percent of an organization's records are more than three years old and are never referred to again. And 75 percent of all correspondence is internal. How much does it cost to find a misfiled document? About a hundred dollars.

Keeping your paper files organized is important. But if something happened to your paper files, you'd probably be able to replace most of the work without too much trouble.

On the other hand, if your computer crashes and the hard drive is wiped out, it could mean losing years of work in the blink of an eye. And unfortunately, computers are almost a necessity in this techno-age; besides, if all you had to work with was an IBM Selectric typewriter, you wouldn't be able to get nearly as much done.

The key to working with computers is to keep your electronic files as organized as your paper files and to regularly back up your work. Why? If you don't have a system that works logically, no one else is going to be able to find anything on your hard drive. And if you don't back up your work, you'll lose everything when your system crashes, which is inevitable.

Here's how to keep your computer files organized:

Keep all of your documents in one place. Even if you're on a network, you should have one place where you keep all of your documents. It could be in your "My Documents" folder or it could be in a folder labeled with your name. Just make sure all of your documents get saved into this location and not in the general C-drive.

Create folders for your major categories of documents. For example, you might have folders for each client, customer, type of product, or people you work for. Consider these folders to be like the hanging folders of your paper filing system.

Within each category of documents, create subfolders. These subfolders will hold your documents. So you might have separate subfolders for "letters," "proposals," "Web site documents," "billing," "phone lists," or whatever it is you work on. When you create a document, you'll save it to the specific subfolder where it belongs. Subfolders are like the manila folders you used to create your filing system.

When your subfolders get too big, divide and conquer. It won't help you stay organized if you have to search through thousands of documents in each subfolder. If your subfolder has more than fifty documents in it, it's probably time to create a new subfolder and move some of the files into it.

Naming Your Files

With early DOS-based systems, you could only give your documents eight-character names. Newer software permits you to name your files almost anything—with more than two hundred characters and spaces in some cases. But if you're not consistent about how you name your files, it won't help you or anyone else find "lost" documents.

If you want to make it easy, use the "8.3" naming system recognized by all DOS-based machines. This system involves choosing a name for your document that is no more than eight characters long (with no spaces), then completing the name with a period followed by a three-character extension. (The extension allows browsers and programs to "recognize" a file and display it correctly.)

But there are only so many words you can spell with eight letters, so this system is rather limited. And computers are just going to get better and more sophisticated in the future. (Think about how many black-and-white monitors you see these days!) So unless your IT department requires you to name your files with the "8.3" system (which they might do if you work for a large corporation that frequently trades files with a European office), try something else.

A better idea is to use the flexibility and sophistication of your computer to identify your documents with a name that's easily remembered, or can be easily searched.

One option is to name by document and date. If you're using the filing system I've outlined here, you're already saving the document to the subfolder where it belongs. While you can add in the name of the client when you're naming a document, it's better to say what the document is, what version it is, and the date it was created. (You can find the date under the "date notes" section when you open up a file, but I find this way to be much easier.)

For example: Letter.v1.0303. This would be the first version of a letter that was created in March 2003.

The nice thing about this naming system is that all of your letters for this client will stay together in the subfolder (they'll be organized alphabetically). Also, if you're searching for all documents created in March 2003, it's easy because you've used periods to separate the important information. (By the way, never use spaces in your computer file names. Use periods instead.)

If you want to add in the client's name, you can put the company's or individual's initials in front of the type of document. For example: IG.Letter.v1.0303. This document would be the first version of a letter for Ilyce Glink, composed in March 2003.

Keep It Short

Whichever way you go with naming your documents, keep it relatively short. When you send files over the Internet, a long name can get gunked up in the transmission, perhaps causing your file to be corrupted or even causing someone else's computer to crash. Also, be aware that some DOS-based systems won't permit anything other than a file with an "8.3" name configuration.

Once you've organized and renamed your files, there are two things you must do regularly to maintain your system: back up your files and defrag your hard drive.

The Only Way to Save Your Stuff

Bob, a grain farmer, has several computers networked in his home. But he recently bought a laptop and was using it to map out his harvest yields. One day, he turned on his computer and the hard drive was fried.

"I lost everything that was on the drive," Bob said. "I should know better. I teach computers."

Fortunately, all of the raw data was saved on his network. But he lost several days of work.

Years ago, backing up a computer system was quite tedious. I can recall spending hours waiting for the system to back up. Today, it's as easy as popping a CD-ROM into a burner, selecting the files you want to save, and burning them onto the CD. You can typically do this in a matter of minutes. There are a few good ways to back up information:

CD-ROM burners. The CD-ROM burners that seem to have the fewest problems and seem to work the best are those that come preinstalled on your computer system. (So make sure you order one with your next computer.) If you're stuck with the computer system you have, you can order a burner and connect it yourself.

Iomega Zip drives. Again, try to get a Zip drive preinstalled on your computer, as they seem to work better and faster and have fewer problems. If you don't get one preinstalled, you can purchase an external Zip drive and install it yourself.

The Internet. Although it's difficult to back up an entire system onto the Internet, it's not impossible, and with bandwidths increasing, it'll get faster and easier. For now, a no-brainer way to back up important individual files is to send them to yourself on the Internet. For example, when my husband,

Sam, needs to back up his Palm, he sends the file to himself. That way, if his system were to crash, he'd have a recent backup of it in his e-mail inbox. Consider creating a free e-mail account at Yahoo! for this purpose.

Plan to back up your system as often as it takes to avoid losing important documents or information. I try to burn a new CD-ROM every week or two. If I lost everything in between it wouldn't be that much work to recreate the documents. If I have an important document I'm working on, like a new book, I might back up that document more frequently.

What if your company frequently backs up your network? Systemwide backups usually work well. But if you have specific documents you don't want to lose, back them up manually, either on Zip disks or CD-ROMs.

Remember to store your backup disks or CDs in a safe location. Billy thought he had a backup system that worked. Each week, he backed up his system and stored the CDs on-site. When his office was destroyed by a fire, he lost everything. Now he backs up his information to a server located more than twenty miles from his office.

(Of course, it's great to back up your system each day, week, or month. But don't forget to frequently save your documents while you're working on them. Computers can crash at any moment, and if they do, you'll probably lose some or all of what you were working on.)

If you're going to use disks to back up your documents, purchase colored disks and designate a separate color for each client, customer, company, or individual. For example, you might back up your boss's documents to a green disk and your documents to a red disk. Be sure to label each disk clearly with what is stored on the disk and the date you made the backup copy.

Quill
suggests

Defragging Your System

Imagine that your computer is a library. Every day, people come to the library. They pull books off the shelf and take them over to a table or easy chair and read them for a while. When they leave, how many will actually put the books away on the shelf where they belong?

Hardly any.

Your computer works the same way. As you use, save, or back up files, they get out of order inside the computer's hard drive—even if you're saving them to the correct subfolder. The way to clear up this mess is to defrag your hard drive. Every once in a while, defrag your hard drive using your system's defragmentation utility software. That way, your hard drive will operate as efficiently as possible.

Money-Saving Tip

Windows and Mac OS operating systems come with basic disk utilities. Or you can purchase products from Norton Utilities (which also makes a great computer and Internet security software). Look for rebates and sales on these items to save money.

Saving and Printing Your E-mails

Creating a paper trail is one of those things we're trained to do. It just seems natural to print every e-mail that appears in your inbox and file it away in a "correspondence" file. But the truth is, you probably don't need to do it. And if your company is large enough, surely your tech people have sent out memos about how you should e-file your e-mail instead of printing it out.

E-filing works pretty well, but it takes some practice. It requires you to keep organized computer files as well as make intelligent decisions about what you can get rid of and what you should keep. Talk to your boss or your IT department for guidelines on saving and naming your e-mail in a way that makes it easy for you to find it in the future.

11 Really Useful Tip

Use Electronic Reminders

Lori, a television producer, uses two kinds of calendars to stay organized. She has a flat paper calendar that she uses to write down which stories she is working on and when they will air, and she also has a Palm, in which she stores her professional and personal information, such as important dates, addresses, and phone numbers.

When something needs to get done, Lori consults her calendars. But she also sets electronic reminders so that even if her written and electronic systems don't match, she's sure not to forget something.

As we've already discussed, you can set up a date file and put notes in each day to remind you of what has to be done, when. But what if you need to remember something three months from now? It's too cumbersome to create a folder with 365 slots in it.

Using an electronic calendar allows you to plant electronic reminders for events far into the future. You can create automatic reminders for yourself so that you always remember Aunt Martha's birthday or your parent's anniversary. I always plug in the dates my taxes are due, the dates my credit card bills have to be paid, and when I need to mail my invoices.

If you don't want to buy a Palm, you can always use a free electronic calendar on the Internet (Yahoo! is one example).

Another plus with this method is that you can access your calendar from anywhere in the world if you have access to the Internet.

Finally, if you use Microsoft software, Microsoft Outlook offers calendar and address database functions. You can easily set electronic reminders inside Outlook that will automatically alert you when the important day or event comes up.

TOP TIPS
for Organizing Your Office

Organization is an ongoing process, and there will be times when you're organized and times when keeping things neat and clean is a huge challenge that drains you of every ounce of energy. Aim to keep things in a reasonably organized state all the time and try to be forgiving if things get out of order from time to time.

Here are some basic tips to help keep things in place:

1. Give each thing its own space. Every item in and around your desk should have its own nook. Magazines should be in magazine holders. Folders that are regularly used should be in a wall rack or drawer where they're easily accessible. Blank paper should be stacked neatly until you're ready to put it in the printer. Your tape, staple remover, paper clips, stapler, pencil sharpener, label maker, and scissors should be kept together in a drawer.

The key is to make sure your spaces are intuitive. If you create a space that isn't logical for the item, people won't automatically go there to find it, and you may have trouble returning the item to its proper place.

2. Put things away immediately. When you were young, your mother probably told you that it was just as easy to hang up your clothes as it was to throw them on the floor. Well, not really, but it takes a lot less energy to hang something up immediately than to pick it up off the floor later on.

The same is true with items on your desk and around your office. When you use the stapler, a pen, or a file, put it away in its proper place when you are finished with it. If you put it away as soon as you are done with it, you'll always know where your stuff is when you need it.

3. File, don't pile. If you push paper for a living, you know it multiplies to the point of seeming to take on a life of its own. If you don't make an immediate decision about what to do with the paper that comes across your desk each day, your pile will start to grow exponentially—as will your stress level.

4. Strive for quality over quantity. Clutter has the unique ability to cloud our thinking. So get rid of whatever is cluttering your office. Let go of papers, files, mementos, and other miscellaneous items that you know you'll never really use. Apply the "KISS" method of organization ("Keep It Simple, Silly"). You'll feel better and your office work won't seem so overwhelming.

CHAPTER 3

Dealing with Customers

Why Customer Service Should Always Be Job #1

Herb Kelleher, the founder of Southwest Airlines, bucks convention in many ways. For example, he has been known to conduct business meetings with a bottle of Wild Turkey in one hand and a pack of smokes in the other.

But he is also unconventional in his thinking about how customers should be treated. For Kelleher, treating the customer as king might actually be a step down from where he thinks customer service should be.

Kelleher believes customers are the most important part of a company. If you have unhappy customers, you can't grow your business and you can't make money. He often says that if you make customers happy, you'll make employees happy. If you make employees happy, shareholders will be happy. And so the entire focus of his business is on making the customer happy by having him or her pay less for better service than he or she could find elsewhere.

(And if you fly Southwest Airlines, you'll now understand why the employees—who own a substantial part of the business—are always smiling.)

Although his business model seems to fly in the face of conventional business school theory (in which you make the employees or the shareholders happy and the customers tag along for the ride), no one can argue it hasn't worked well for Southwest Airlines. The company remains *the* most profitable airline in the United States, the *only* airline that has never had a losing quarter, *and* the only airline that has never had to lay off or furlough employees—even after the terrorist attacks on September 11, 2001.

So what is Kelleher actually doing? He is catering to his customers. His company spends a ton of time finding future employees. The company receives more than two hundred thousand applications each year, and Kelleher has trained his human resources department to search for people with the right attitude about customers and life itself. Kelleher believes you need to find people with good minds and attitudes. Any job can be taught. Having a bad attitude can easily get you fired. But if you have the right attitude, and you're hardworking and smart, you can get promoted all the way to the top.

Before you whip out your resumé to start revising it to send to Southwest, consider how the Kelleher lessons in customer service might be applied to the company you work for.

Every business needs customers (paying customers, preferably), and plenty of them. Does your company believe customers come first? Or is the emphasis on employees or shareholders (or on the individuals who founded and own the business)?

It's difficult to always put customers or clients first. It takes time and energy away from trying to get your work done. But maybe there's something to Kelleher's "crazy" belief that if you satisfy your customers, you'll also satisfy your employees, as well as those who have invested money in the business.

In this chapter, we'll look at different ways to put customers first, and how you can help polish your company's customer service.

12 Really Useful Tip

Cultivate Your Customer Base

According to the Marketing Resource Alliance, the typical company gets 65 percent of its business from existing customers. Finding a new customer costs five times as much as keeping an existing one happy.

In many companies, you'll get 80 percent of your business from 20 percent of your clients. If you can't keep these people happy, you'll soon be out of business. Here are eight ways to keep your existing customers feeling satisfied:

1. Provide an excellent product or service, and charge less than the competition. Glen, a mortgage broker in southern California, says all of his business is from repeat customers and referrals. Why? In addition to providing loans for home improvement projects, his company helps customers design their project and screen contractors at no extra charge. And all fees are disclosed up front. The company has an employee whose title is "director of initial impressions." A large part of his job is meeting people at the door and welcoming them in by name.

2. Be honest with your customers, particularly if you're running late on a project or deadline. If there's a problem, let the customer know immediately. At Southwest Airlines, you get information about plane delays almost as soon as the check-in staff finds out. Hiding a delay or a problem almost always comes back to bite you. Dennis says misinformation and unmet expectations are the name of the game in his industry. His Dallas-based telecommunications company services small to midsized companies. To differentiate his firm, Dennis's employees have a mandate to always tell the truth, whether the news is good or bad.

3. Get regular feedback from your customers. Business consultants say that too few companies ever ask their clients or customers if they're happy with the goods or services they're receiving and if they like the price they're paying. "If you don't ask, you won't know," said Pauline, a consultant in southern California. She noted that a recent study of thirty-eight thousand customers of twenty-five large Canadian companies concluded that customers who tell you what and how you can do better are your more loyal customers. "If you listen to what they say and take action on their recommendations, they will keep coming back," she noted. As a bonus, you may be surprised by how useful the suggestions actually are.

4. Give service with a smile. The old cliché is true: It's easier to catch flies with honey than with vinegar. No matter how tired or cranky you are, practice smiling and being cheerful. If someone asks you how you are, tell him or her you're "great" or "wonderful." Your good attitude will make others feel good around you, and, as a bonus, if you say you feel good enough times, you'll start to believe it.

5. Stay in touch. It's cheaper to stay in touch with current clients than to find new ones. Even if your product is one that will only be bought "once in a lifetime," your existing customers have friends and family they could recommend—if they've had a good experience. Good ways to stay in touch include customer surveys, newsletters, periodic postcards, and holiday greeting cards.

6. Educate your customer. Explain how the process will work. Give quotes or fees for goods and services in writing. Talk about how long it will take to complete the job or provide the product. Encourage your customer to ask plenty of questions and to feel free to call anytime with further questions or comments.

Staying in touch with your customers and clients throughout the year allows you to deepen your contacts—and perhaps grow your business. Create your own cards to say thank you or "We appreciate your business." Avery offers single-sized card packs and envelopes that work with the card-making program at AmericanGreetings.com and other greeting card or publishing programs. Epson offers photo greeting cards that allow you to put any digital image on the front and create a personal message on the inside. Or you can send Masterpiece Studio cards that simply say, "We appreciate your business" and laser-print a personal message inside. Quill even offers custom printing. See Quill.com for details on dozens of options.

7. Ask for referrals. If you work with one division of a company, and you're sure they're satisfied with your product, service, and price, you might ask if there is another division in the company that might benefit from your services. The cheapest way to grow your business is to have someone refer a customer to you.

8. Find an "influencer." If you need a real-estate attorney, you'll probably ask your real-estate agent and your friends for a few names. If you're looking for a new hair salon, you'll probably ask a friend. The real-estate agent and the friend are "influencers," or people who influence your decision to buy a product or use a service. If you're looking to cultivate your customer base, find people or companies in complementary businesses that service customers who could benefit from your product or service. For example, if you're a home inspector or mortgage lender or real-estate attorney, you'll want to form an alliance with a real-estate brokerage firm so you can trade prospective clients and customers.

Carie, a book publisher in New York, says people need to hear about a book an average of seven separate times before they will purchase a copy. So if an author gets on the *Today Show* and is seen by seven million people on a single day, those people still need to hear about the book six other times before they'll place an order at Amazon.com or at their local bookstore.

Cultivating your customer base works the same way by:

Priming the pump. Staying in touch with customers conditions them to purchase your product or service. It reminds them you're around.

Putting your company top of mind. Perhaps there are other companies that provide a similar product or service. By cultivating your customer base, you establish your company as the leading company.

Lowering resistance to your products or services. It's one thing to ask a customer or client for their business. It's another thing to ask them to make a switch from a current provider (where they already know the good, the bad, and the ugly) to a new company. A prospective client or customer is much more likely to switch over if he or she has not only heard from you, but has also heard about you from current customers.

Bonus Tip

More than twenty-five years ago, I spent four weeks at an overnight camp called Sanborn in the Colorado Rockies. My sisters spent a summer or two there as well. Each of us felt it was a fabulous, life-changing experience.

Ever since, the camp has sent each of us a birthday card, a gentle yet effective reminder that the camp is still there. It's the best possible customer cultivation—clearly, I'm not going back to camp (though I wish I could), but the owners are betting I'll have children of my own someday (in fact, I have two). The camp is hoping that one day I'll be ready to send my kids away for a life-changing summer too, and I'll think about the good times I had at Sanborn and choose to send them there. If I can afford it, I probably will.

If you're going to do it right, customer cultivation is itself a long-term business. To succeed, you not only have to do everything right, but you also have to remind prospective customers of how valuable your products and services are over a long period of time.

13 Really Useful Tip

Refine Your Customer Service

Are you surprised when you receive really great customer service? I am—mostly because it doesn't happen too often anymore. What many companies don't understand or have forgotten in this age of deals and bargains is that great customer service often gives you a customer for life.

Great customer service was once a hallmark of a terrific business. And I still think it is. My sons attend a day camp that delivers some of the best customer service I've ever seen. From the moment you sign up, there is constant contact with the camp staff: newsletters, brochures, birthday and holiday cards, literature for parents, postcards from counselors, and even a video of the previous summer's fun.

But customer service isn't just about sending stuff in the mail. It's the ability to listen and respond to what your customers are saying. My sons' camp knows that both their parents work, so it offers a hot-lunch program. Camp tuition is expensive, so it offers several ways to pay and even extends a discount to those who pay in full by a certain date. If you have a question about your child, or a concern about the staff, someone is always available to talk with you about the situation and find the answer you seek.

In short, it's the kind of customer service that is so rare you're taken aback when you get it. And it generates loyalty.

What kind of service are your customers receiving? In general, great customer service depends on three qualities: it should be *responsive, reliable,* and *respectful.* If it isn't, and your surveys aren't coming back with only "excellent" and "good" checked off, there's probably room for improvement. Here are a few ways you can give your customers better service:

Give your customers what they want—the first time. When I go to my mechanic, I want fast service, honest service, and a decent price. When I first started taking my car to my service station eight years ago, service was spotty. Sometimes you got a good guy and sometimes you got a jerk. If you got a jerk, you had to waste time complaining or micromanaging the repair. If it wasn't for the supreme convenience of the place, I would have searched for a new service station. So I complained. But I wasn't the only one complaining, and the management was listening. My service station has dramatically improved its customer service in the past few years. Now every visit is terrific, and I no longer question whether I'm getting what I pay for.

What do your customers want? Identify the top two or three things that are most important to them. Then make sure they get it the first time—not after they've complained.

Treat old customers like new ones. Karen, a customer service representative for a cosmetics company, was bothered by a new program her company started that rewarded first-time users at twice the rate of existing customers. That seemed wrong to her, she recalls thinking, because regular customers might order only once or twice a year. She knew her instincts were right when existing customers saw advertisements about the program and called to complain that they were being treated unfairly. They wanted to be rewarded too! After Karen spent a whole day on the phone, she suggested to her superior that the promotion be extended to all customers. The rewards program was extended to everyone, and Karen's business doubled.

Often companies take old customers for granted. But it's far less expensive to keep an existing client than to find a new one.

In fact, some studies report that it costs just a quarter to keep an existing client for every dollar it costs to find a new one. That kind of savings can certainly improve any company's bottom line.

Don't let your customers question your honesty. Some companies, like airlines, offer less expensive pricing on the Internet than you can get through their toll-free number or in person. If you're offering different pricing strategies through different media (telephone, Internet, mail, etc.), make everyone aware of where they can go to get the best price.

If you're not honest with your customers all the time, they'll start to question your truthfulness or will stop believing what you tell them entirely. And if that happens, you might as well toss your customer service program out the window.

Aim to exceed their expectations. Companies with successful customer service programs focus on exceeding the expectations their customers have for their product or service. You don't need to lower the bar to do this. What you should do is identify the expectations your customers have. For example, they might want good service in a timely fashion at a fair price. If you then deliver excellent service (with a smile) in a timely fashion at the best price in town, your business should thrive.

Be cheerful. No one wants to talk to a customer service representative who is in a foul mood or who makes it abundantly clear that he or she has far better things to do at that moment. If your reps don't have a smile on their faces or kindness in their voices, they aren't giving customers the informed, attentive, cheerful, polite, and helpful service that will leave the positive impression you're hoping for.

Make sure every rep has the same information. If you call the Internal Revenue Service with a question about your return, you will get an answer. But if you call back five times, you could end up with six different answers. That hardly inspires confidence in a taxpayer.

It works the same in any business. Don't let your customer service reps give different answers to the same question, or you could wind up losing the trust and respect of your customer or client.

Remember that happy customers spread the word. In 1951, Lillian Vernon started her mail-order company from her apartment in Mount Vernon, New York. She likes to say that everything she needed to know about selling she learned at her kitchen table. She believes the foundation of a successful business is customer loyalty, and she views every one of her twenty-one million customers as a "real" person. One of her rules of thumb is that a happy customer may tell three others about what you have to offer. An unhappy customer will tell ten others about the bad experience.

The customer may not always be right. But you should treat customers with respect at all times and strive to make them as happy as possible. The result could be three new customers, instead of ten new customers for your competitor.

For more tips on improving customer service, see page 85.

Bonus Tip

Simply changing the name of your customer service department doesn't mean you're automatically going to deliver better results. Calling your staff "customer care representatives" without implementing a new strategy to go along with the name change doesn't change what they are; in fact, the name change could backfire if your customers expect to be better cared for and still get the same poor service. If you're going to change the name of this department, make sure you change the customer service culture as well.

14 Really Useful Tip

Polish Up on Customer Etiquette

Some days, it seems as if basic etiquette is just a quaint notion from bygone years.

Drivers often barely pause at a stop sign, and sometimes ignore it altogether—which is not only rude, but also downright dangerous. Rarely does anyone offer a seat to a pregnant woman or elderly passenger on a train or bus. Even a heartfelt "please" or "thank you" seems rare.

While it might be put up with in casual everyday encounters, poor etiquette doesn't fly with customers, and they'll stop using your services or products if they don't receive treatment that is polite and fair.

Telephone Etiquette

Although most people these days are accustomed to leaving detailed messages for people on voice mail, every now and then a real live person answers when you call a company, and it almost seems intrusive to ask them to take a message. The telephone is one of your most important tools, and there are proper rules for telephone conduct, whether you're answering a call, talking to someone's voice mail, or actually speaking to the person you've been looking for. Here are some pointers on telephone etiquette:

Answer quickly. No one likes to wait through seemingly endless rings before someone finally answers the phone. It makes you feel like you're calling a radio station to try to win concert tickets!

Answer by identifying yourself or your company. When I answer my phone, I say, "This is Ilyce." I can do this because I own my own company, and I'm the one who always answers the phone. You may be able to answer with your name, if it's a private extension, or with the name of your department ("Human resources. Can I help you?"). Of course, that wouldn't have worked for Libby. She was the receptionist in a law firm for more than thirty years. In the early years of the firm, she would answer "7606," which were the last four digits of the firm's phone number. Later on, she would simply answer with the firm's name.

Answer politely and cheerfully. Whatever is going on in your personal life, don't bring it to the office, and don't project it onto whoever is calling. It's also polite to ask, "How may I help you?"

Avoid using hold. It's fine to put someone on hold for a minute if they don't mind. But check back in with the customer every thirty to forty-five seconds to see if he or she wants to continue holding. It's better to take the person's name and number and forward that information on to the right person. Taking the caller's name and number not only frees up the person's time—it also helps you better manage yours.

Speak slowly and clearly. If you go too fast, it's possible that numbers and names will be confused, which will create errors that require more time and attention to fix. Repeat all phone numbers twice.

Identify yourself when you make a call. Always leave your full name, your company's name, and a number or extension. If the person loses the message but remembers your name or your company's name, he or she can track you down.

Remember that Caller ID has got your number. So don't be rude and simply hang up if you dial incorrectly.

E-mail Etiquette

Alice, a book agent in New York, has noticed that using e-mail has dramatically cut down on the time she spends on the phone. It has also made her far more productive. She can answer e-mails late at night or early in the morning from home. And she can have her administrative assistant, Stephanie, answer them for her if she is out of town or at a meeting.

If you're using e-mail to communicate with your boss, your colleagues, or the outside world, here are a few tips on e-mail etiquette:

Keep it short. An e-mail is supposed to take the place of a quick phone call. It doesn't usually replace a formal letter (although you can attach one to your e-mail). By nature, it's meant to be short and to the point.

Don't be cutesy. In a business e-mail, don't include smiley faces or quotes that reflect your personal philosophy of life. Save that for the e-mail you send to family and friends.

Check for grammar and spelling mistakes. Most e-mail programs have grammar-check and spell-check programs. Use them.

Answer your e-mail quickly. Or, if a response is going to take time, hit the "reply" button and say that you are working on it and will get back to the person as soon as possible.

Office Etiquette

If a customer or client visits your office, don't make him or her feel like an intruder. Instead, be welcoming. Offer a cup of coffee or water. Invite the client or customer to sit in a comfortable chair while waiting. If you make the customer or client feel welcome and special, it will only add to his or her comfort with your company's products or services.

Handling Complaints

If it's your job to handle complaints for your department or company, you could be getting an earful every day. The best way to handle these calls or e-mails is to not take it personally and to remember how you feel when you call a company to complain about a product or service.

Be polite. Listen intently to the caller's problem. Take notes (preferably on your computer). Reassure the person that the problem will be taken care of and that the appropriate people will be notified. And be sure to get the caller's name and telephone number.

15 Really Useful Tip

Learn How to Deal with Difficult Customers and Clients

Difficult customers and clients can be angry, impatient, demanding, talkative (well, usually they're yelling), or perhaps indecisive. Why are some customers and clients difficult? It's usually due to one of several reasons:

✓ The customer or client feels that he or she is the most important person in the world, and everyone else is just wasting his or her time. Obviously, this isn't rational, and you're not going to change it. The good news is it's not a personal attack.

✓ The customer or client is having trouble at home, or is sick, or has a spouse or child who is sick. You have no way of knowing this (unless the person informs you of it). However, it could cause the customer or client to display uneven behavior—sometimes nice, sometimes not nice.

✓ The client's hands are tied on his or her side. If you're getting squeezed, it could be because the customer is getting squeezed or is frustrated with the way the deal is turning out.

✓ The customer is in financial trouble at home, or his or her business is in trouble. Being difficult might be a way for this customer to delay payment for services rendered or products purchased.

✓ The customer has not had his or her expectations met in the past. This person might be thinking that the more demanding he is, the better service he'll receive. Of course, the opposite is true.

✓ The customer feels frustrated because of communication problems he or she is having with you or your company.

No matter why a customer or client is difficult, the most important thing is that you try to diffuse the situation. An angry customer is more likely to say negative things about your company and will go out of his or her way to steer other companies or customers away from doing business with you.

If you can diffuse the situation and turn the customer around, it's a win-win situation for everyone. Remember: a little goodwill goes a long way. Here are some ways you can work with a difficult customer:

Remember that the customer is right until proven otherwise. Always assume the customer is telling the truth until you have proof otherwise. And let the customer know you believe him or her. Being agreeable is one way to diffuse a difficult situation.

Listen carefully. Anne works for a radio station in Atlanta. She is the front line of defense when people call to (occasionally) praise or (usually) complain about what they're hearing on the air. She very politely listens, notes their complaint, takes their name and number (if appropriate), and hangs up.

Be understanding. Make an effort to understand the customer's point of view. Perhaps there is a problem that is only visible from the other side of the table.

Work on solving the problem. Most problems usually have some sort of solution or remedy. Sometimes you have to (nicely!) adjust the customer's expectations or perhaps say thank you or apologize. Ask the customer how he or she would like you to solve the problem. You might get the solution handed to you in ten seconds.

Follow up. Make sure you check in with the customer down the line (or have your boss do it). This way, you'll know the customer's problem has been solved and you'll show him or her that solving the problem was important to you.

Finally, remember that it isn't your fault. If a customer is difficult, it's typically because he or she is angry at the situation, not at you. If you can keep from feeling that the customer is attacking you personally, you'll have an easier time dealing with the situation.

Bonus Tip

Don't underestimate the power of an apology. Saying "I'm sorry" is the easiest and fastest way to calm down a customer who's blowing off steam. Remember: it costs more to find a new customer than to keep an existing one.

Protecting Your Boss

Sometimes difficult customers will insist on speaking with your boss. If your boss is okay with that, fine. But most of the time, you'll want to protect your boss from getting the earful this customer wants to give. You can do this by being firm, yet polite, with callers. Make sure the caller knows that you've passed along his or her message or that you will find out the information he or she is seeking. Keep your tone neutral and make sure the customer knows the buck stops with you.

Julie, an administrative assistant, says she firmly tells repeat callers that her boss can't be interrupted. Every time they call back, she tells them she has passed along the message. At the end of the day, she asks her boss what he wants to do about a persistent caller. Then, she handles the call.

"It isn't always a pleasant way to end the day, but I just try to remind myself that this isn't about me. It's about an unpleasant situation."

16 Really Useful Tip

Say Thank You in Creative Ways

It's nice to say thank you to customers and clients, but often words aren't enough. For a big piece of business, a gift might be in order. And it might be up to you to think of a creative way for your boss or your company to say thank you to a client or customer.

How do you choose a good gift? The best gifts are tailored to the recipient. It could be related to a hobby (golf, cooking, travel), something to do with business (pen-and-pencil set, desk accessories), or a fun way to spend personal time (gift certificates to spas, restaurants, gourmet food companies). The best gifts are creative, unexpected, and fun.

Here are some different categories of gifts, along with some of the companies and Web sites that provide these items. This list is by no means inclusive, and I'm not necessarily recommending these companies or sites (though I have used quite a few), but it should get your brain working in a different direction.

If in the course of doing business you come across a company that provides unique and creative gifts, list them in the gift log at the end of this section for easy reference.

Monogrammed Gifts

Baseball caps, shirts, aprons, jackets, sweatshirts, dress shirts, golf apparel, card holders, pen-and-pencil sets, stationary, towels, picture frames

✓ Monogrammed apparel (LandsEnd.com, Sam's Club)
✓ Monogrammed silver items (Tiffany's)
✓ Monogrammed towels (LandsEnd.com, NeimanMarcus.com)
✓ Monogrammed pen-and-pencil sets (Mont Blanc)

Food Gifts

✓ Gourmet steaks (OmahaSteaks.com, SteaksandSeafood.com, Chicagogourmetsteaks.com)
✓ Chocolates (Godiva.com, Sees.com)
✓ Fruit (HarryandDavid.com, citrusgifts.com, Fruit of the Month Club)
✓ Cheese (WilliamsSonoma.com, GrahamCheese.com, CheeseandWine.com, HarryandDavid.com)
✓ Turkeys and hams (Honeybaked.com)
✓ Cookies (MrsFields.com, TheCookieCutters.com)
✓ Catered dinners
✓ Wine (purchase for local clients or check state laws· on sending wine by mail)

Books

Amazon.com, BarnesandNoble.com

Cultural Gifts

Tickets to a museum show, a play, an opera, a symphony, a concert, or a sporting event

Cool Office Gifts

HammacherSchlemmer.com, EddieBauer.com, LandsEnd.com, SharperImage.com

Gift Certificates

For local restaurants, shops, day spas, massage centers, or book-stores. For the customer who loves gardening, give a gift certifi-cate to a flower company (MichiganBulbs.com)

Personal Gifts

Candles, soaps, skincare products (PotteryBarn.com, H2Oplus.com)

Gifts That Work

Gift	Supplier	Cost

Giving Don'ts

There are certain things you shouldn't give to a customer or client. Above all, never give anything that would send the wrong message.

Don't give anything too personal. Perfume and clothing don't usually sit well with clients or customers. It just feels wrong to give such a gift to a business or professional contact. If you feel that a client would enjoy something like that, give a gift certificate to a local department store instead.

Don't give anything tasteless. Gag gifts that could cause hurt feelings or embarrassment aren't appropriate in office settings.

Don't give anything religious. It's too personal, and you might assume the client or customer practices one religion when they really practice another or none at all.

While gifts for clients are important, don't forget to reward your own team. Recognize exceptional efforts with award plaques, a box of pens or pencils with the employee's name on them, or gift certificates to a favorite store.

Giving Dos

There are other things that make a gift special besides the amount of money you spend on it.

Wrapping counts. A beautifully wrapped gift usually makes a positive impression, no matter what is inside.

Personally sign the card. If your gift is beautifully wrapped but you enclose a preprinted card, the gift will be discounted slightly in the customer's mind. Make sure you sign the card yourself.

Choose a nonstandard time of year to give a gift. We often think of the winter holidays and New Year's as the right time to give a gift to a client or customer. But everyone sends things around that time of year. To stand out from the crowd, consider giving gifts on your company's anniversary, the client's anniversary of working with your company, or a holiday like Labor Day, the Fourth of July, or the Chinese New Year.

Consider donating to a charity in a customer's name. Some clients and customers may appreciate a donation made in their name to a charity, or a tree planted in their name, or even a Habitat for Humanity house built in their name. One company started putting the money they would have spent on gifts for clients into a local charity that helps needy children get warm clothes for winter and toys at Christmas. Each employee is given money to shop for a particular child, and then each client is sent a letter about a particular child and what the employee bought for him or her. The program has been well received by the firm's clients and staff.

Choose something unusual. If purchasing chocolates or cookies seems unoriginal, try an unusual food product or food basket. For example, you can send a Georgia Peach Basket of gourmet foods that are all made with peaches. Or try a kit that teaches you how to make boiled peanuts. If you know the client has kids, you might give a gift that the client and his or her children can enjoy, such as holiday cookies in a can.

Loyalty Programs

One of the best ways to say thank you is to do it year-round. Loyalty programs, like airline miles or cash-back awards from credit card companies, help build brands and keep customers coming back.

Consider these different types of reward programs:

✓ Discounts on future purchases (20 percent off your next purchase over $200)

✓ Coupons for bonus items (buy a set of pans and get a frying pan free)

✓ Free items with a purchase that reaches a certain dollar amount (get a free book if you spend $250 or more)

✓ Reward points that build up over time (when you reach five hundred points, you get two items for the price of one)

✓ Incentives for referrals (get 20 percent off your next purchase each time you refer a new customer)

Bonus Tip

The best way to be creative with a thank you is to do it when it's least expected. Sometimes the element of surprise increases the pleasure the recipient feels when opening your gift.

You can also inspire customer loyalty simply by treating your customers better than your competitor treats its customers. Consider sending birthday or anniversary cards (paper or electronic) and a personally written thank-you note after a particularly large purchase.

TOP TIPS

for Improving Customer Service

Think about why you might buy something from one store over another. It usually boils down to convenience, selection, and price. But if all of those things are equal, you'll probably go to the merchant who gives you fabulous customer service. In fact, you might forgo price or convenience just to get personalized customer service.

Now turn that around and apply it to your own customers. How can you improve their experience?

1. Team up with colleagues to brainstorm ways to improve customer service. Putting your heads together may help you dream up creative ways of making your customers or clients happier.

2. Create a customer service focus group. Invite ten or twenty of your most loyal customers to meet with you regularly to give you ideas and input on how to improve your customer service. Ask them what kind of service they're looking for.

3. Stay in regular contact. Send out handwritten notes or preprinted cards, offer free subscriptions, send e-mail updates, and follow up after a project ends. Customer survey forms are useful—let your customers know that if they can't check "excellent" next to every question, you'll be in touch to find out why.

4. Always be polite. It's business, not personal. Take a calm, confident approach that will put your customer or client at ease. Apologize for any mistake that was made and be up-front about taking responsibility.

5. Don't create false expectations. Instead, promise less and deliver more, on time and under budget.

6. Let your customers help you build your business. Create a referral form and send it to your clients or customers with your invoice. Offer them a discount on future services if they refer clients to you.

7. Put yourself in your customer's shoes. Your clients and customers may not see your business the way you do—and they may not understand everything that happens behind the scenes. These days, transparency counts, so take the time to educate your customer on how your business works.

Bonus Tip

Quill's vice president of customer relations spends his day acting as the customer's advocate. It's his job to make sure that the customer's order is placed correctly. What does Quill think is good customer service? Exceeding the customer's expectations every time. And, when something happens that shouldn't, making sure the same mistake doesn't happen again. His best advice? "Ask the customer what it is they want you to do to fix the problem. Ninety-nine percent of the time, they will tell you exactly what needs to be done, and that in itself solves the problem. I listen to them, then restate what they've just told me to make sure I have it right," explains Ken Wnek. "Then I just go ahead and fix it."

CHAPTER 4

Improving Office Relationships

Getting Along with Your Office Mates Goes a Long Way toward Making Your Office Run Better

Every place of business has its share of office drama. It could be a boss who plays favorites, or a jealous coworker, or a mean-spirited colleague who sabotages success.

Patty had someone like that working for her. Whatever project they were working on, Ron just didn't want to cooperate. He would delay and delay and delay until everyone got yelled at or the project got canceled. Patty tried to help Ron integrate better into the office community, but in the end she had to fire him. His poor attitude and performance were starting to make her look bad to her own bosses.

Because life is unfair, the bad guys don't always get fired—sometimes they get promoted and you have to report to them! In Hollywood there's a saying: Be nice to your secretary, because she could soon be your boss.

You should make an effort to get along with your office mates not only because you could wind up reporting to them. Toning down the office tension and politics will make everyone happier and more productive. If you expend energy on in-house fighting, you won't have enough creativity left to expand your responsibilities and take on new projects.

The bottom line is, your office will run better and be a nicer place to work if everyone makes an effort to get along. In this chapter, I'll give you some suggestions on how to make your office run better.

Bonus Tip

What makes a good leader? It isn't a job title. Quill's project leader of organizational development sent me this list of nine qualities every leader should have:

1. Vision. You have to know where you're going.
2. The ability to inspire trust in those who work with you and for you.
3. The ability to let your employees and coworkers be part of the decision-making process, where appropriate.
4. The ability to share power. You can't operate under the myth that you have all the power and that's all that matters.
5. Great listening skills. You need to solicit feedback along the way from those individuals who are working for you.
6. The ability to praise others, where appropriate. Great leaders positively reinforce those who work for them, both individually and in teams.
7. The ability to set clear expectations so that when employees and coworkers walk into work every day, they know what you need.
8. The ability to share knowledge. You have to let people know what's going on in the business and how each individual can make a difference.
9. The ability to impart technical knowledge. Take what you've learned and find a way to pass it on.

17 Really Useful Tip

Learn How to Motivate Your Colleagues and Build a Strong Team

There are good managers and there are bad managers, and if you work long enough, you'll probably experience both. Good managers have the all-important skills necessary to keep their employees and colleagues motivated and focused. Bad managers just stumble through, failing to inspire the confidence necessary to succeed.

There are several key traits all good managers have:

Strong communication skills. Good managers have the ability to clearly tell people what they want and what they expect their employees to do in a certain time frame. Unfortunately, it's a fairly rare skill. Another rare skill is the ability to listen.

Respect for everyone. Whether my father, an attorney who represented various municipalities, was speaking to a village president or the janitor at Village Hall, he treated everyone with the same kindness and respect. It made everyone want to do his or her best for him.

Secure personality. Good managers have the ability to encourage others to do their best, even if it means developing skills that exceed those of the manager. Insecure people have a hard time encouraging success because they're always worried about losing control.

Ability to see the big picture. Someone has to keep his or her eye on the prize. A good manager always sees the light at the end of the tunnel and the road you need to ride to get there.

Ability to give it to you straight. Whether the news is good or bad, a good manager gives it to you straight, in a way that is conscious of your feelings.

You don't have to be a manager to help motivate your colleagues. But if you're in charge of a particular project, there are a few things you can do to make everyone feel focused and like he or she is a part of the team:

Be productive. Motivating others is easier if people see you happy and productive. Just as having a good boss can teach you how to be good boss, being enthusiastic about your job can motivate others to do the same.

Understand what drives your colleagues. Is it family, friends, recognition, public service, a need to learn new things? What motivates you? Ann says she is motivated to do a good job because she feels lucky to work in a supportive environment.

Liberally sprinkle praise. Everyone likes to feel as if they're doing a good job. An unexpected compliment will help your colleagues feel good about their contributions.

Listen closely. Your colleagues may offer suggestions you hadn't thought of.

Set smarter goals, for yourself and others. All of us are goal oriented. We like starting a project and completing it successfully. But if the goal isn't sharply in focus, it will be easy to get sidetracked. Make sure your project goals are specific, measurable, and realistic, that they stretch the minds of those involved, and that they are in line with corporate objectives.

Raising Office Morale

It's not surprising that employees and employers see workplace issues differently. In several studies that took place over three decades, employees were asked to rank ten things they wanted from their jobs in order of importance. In the most recent version of the study, conducted by the NOVA Group, the employees ranked each item as follows:

Interesting work
Appreciation and recognition
Feeling "in on things"
Job security
Good wages
Promotion/growth
Good working conditions
Personal loyalty
Tactful discipline
Sympathetic help with problems

Employers were then asked to guess how their employees ranked those items. Here's how they assumed their employees ranked them:

Good wages
Job security
Promotion/growth
Good working conditions
Interesting work
Personal loyalty
Tactful discipline
Appreciation and recognition
Sympathetic help with problems
Feeling "in on things"

Clearly, employers and employees are not on the same page, and that can destabilize office morale.

Terri Levine used to be miserable working. She was president of a national healthcare corporation and made a ton of money, but she didn't feel like she was doing something she was passionate about. Her work, which would have been fascinating to someone else, didn't really interest her.

She became a company coach (her Web site is www.ComprehensiveCoachingU.com) and is hired by corporations around the world to identify workplace issues that are making employees unhappy and solutions to change a company's culture so employees are happier. She even wrote a book called *Work Yourself Happy,* which includes tips on how to be happier at work.

One thing she's discovered is that if employers aren't open to improving the lives of their employees and colleagues, it's more difficult to make changes for the better.

In one case, Terri was asked by an employer to come in and find ways to improve profitability and productivity. She conducted confidential interviews with fifteen line employees and six managers. After looking at everyone's comments, she found that all of the employees were unhappy. When she came back to the owner with her results, he said, "I couldn't care less if people are happy."

Unfortunately, Terri said, "One out of every five companies that approach me really doesn't care about its employees."

If office morale is a problem where you work, take some of these steps to identify the source of the negative feelings and take action:

- ✓ Ask your colleagues why they're unhappy. Are they overworked and underpaid? Or do they feel unappreciated? What do they want and what do they need?
- ✓ Get beyond unrealistic suggestions. If someone says she wants ten weeks of vacation, you have to probe deeper to figure out what that person is really trying to tell you. Perhaps she's feeling stressed out or incapable of hitting targets and goals that have been set.
- ✓ Talk to your boss. If you've noticed that office morale is a problem, it's likely your boss has noticed as well. Make an appointment to talk with your boss (or human resources) about the problem and what could be done to improve morale.
- ✓ Create an anonymous company-wide suggestion box. Encourage your colleagues and coworkers to drop in suggestions for improving the workplace environment.

18 Really Useful Tip

Take Action to Resolve Conflicts

There's a group of workers in one office in Oregon who can't seem to get along. They fight about everything, from making the morning coffee to going home early to signing up for vacation time.

As a worker in this environment, such behavior would be not only unsettling, but also demoralizing. Who would feel motivated to get up in the morning and go to work when you had to face such an environment every day? Productivity is also at stake: if a disagreement turns into a screaming match, no one gets any work done for the next few hours.

Why do people fight over making coffee when there's a gourmet coffee shop around each corner (or in the lobby)? The answer tends to be one of the following reasons:

Insecurity. Like a dog guarding its yard, some office workers will go all out to protect their "territory." Mostly, that's an expression of insecurity. They believe that if they allow someone to cross the threshold of their territory, that person will figure out that they are expendable. They're insecure about themselves or their job, so they hold on to every task they do as if it could vanish overnight.

Stress. Whether self-induced or office-induced, stress can make us rather grumpy and difficult to get along with. Relieving the pressure can vastly reduce the number of conflicts in your office. (See chapter 7 for a number of suggestions on how to relieve stress at the office.)

Control. There are some people who like to control every situation. It reminds me a little of how kids act in grade school. Someone takes charge and tries to make everyone else go along with whatever he or she decides. In an office situation, control and power often go hand in hand (unfortunately for the rest of us).

Recognition. It may sound silly, but some people will pick a fight in the office simply so that other colleagues will pay attention to him or her. It's far better to be recognized for high-quality work than high-maintenance behavior, but some coworkers believe any recognition is better than none at all.

Fairness. Everyone knows that life isn't fair, but apparently some people don't think that this doctrine applies to office life. My friend Ralph once worked for a law firm where partners would regularly count the ceiling tiles in the offices to be sure that every partner got exactly the same amount of square feet (one ceiling tile measured twelve inches by twelve inches, or one square foot). Ralph, who couldn't care less about the size of his office as long as it had a telephone, a computer, room for photos of his wife and kids, and a small CD player, thought this was hilarious. Then again, according to another partner in the firm, he had about three extra square feet in his office!

Mediating a Dispute

Some people might say, "Stay out of it. Helen and Lorraine have been fighting for years." But if you're trying to get work done, the squabbling of coworkers can make the office an uncomfortable place to be. Here's how you can help mediate a dispute without finding yourself squeezed in the middle:

Identify the problem. Why are your coworkers quarreling? Talk to both sides of the dispute and try to see the issue at hand from both perspectives. Avoid laying blame, and try to get both sides to avoid blaming each other.

Encourage the parties to talk to each other about the real problem, not the superficial issue. A fight over who is going to make the morning coffee could be about decaf versus regular, or it could be a symptom of a long-term power struggle. Try to learn as much as possible about the needs of all the parties involved, as well as any external factors that can be pushing the situation. Make sure everyone keeps his or her emotions in check.

Come up with a solution that has something for everyone. When you're buying or selling a home, the best deal is the one in which everyone walks away happy from the closing table. In the case of the decaf versus regular fight, the answer could be as easy as purchasing a separate coffeemaker for decaf (or stronger, or flavored) coffee. If the real issue is a power struggle, the solution may be more elusive. Just remember that everyone has to feel like a winner if you're going to solve the problem for good.

Resolving conflicts takes confidence, skill, and kindness. And if you're able to do it, your colleagues will thank you.

What to do if you're the problem. It's likely that at some point in your career, someone is going to have a problem with you or how you've handled a situation or project. First, don't take it personally. Remember: this is work, not first grade. Next, try to be objective about the other person's criticism (even if it's not given in a particularly helpful way). Is there any truth to it? Try to be open to someone else's recommendations for improvement.

Finally, take some time before you respond. Your initial reaction might be to lash out angrily instead of thinking things through. It's better to take some time to cool down (a quick walk around the block might help) before you respond to any criticisms or accusations.

19 Really Useful Tip

Improve Communication by Keeping People in the Loop

A study by the International Association of Business Communicators (IABC) Research Foundation, and sponsored by the accounting firm Deloitte and Touche, investigated the connection between how well companies communicate and how much success they enjoy.

"Communication Competence and Business Success: A Comparative Review of Communication Programs" found that companies with a higher level of communication focused on four key areas: clarity of purpose, effective interfaces, effective information sharing, and the communication behavior of leaders.

The study concluded that the most successful companies encouraged the free flow of information from top to bottom. All employees, from CEO to secretary to sales rep, should understand and be aligned with the company's overall business strategy. The study also found that people at all organizational levels can learn from one another.

Keeping People in the Loop

Here are some things you can do to improve communication and keep people in the loop.

> **Bonus Tip**
>
> *Parade* magazine recently published a list of suggestions for e-mail etiquette. They suggest you respond quickly, refrain from sending junk e-mails, and watch what you write (profanity is never a good idea). Often, e-mails contain misspellings and sloppy writing, which make you look bad, so use your spell-check program before you hit send. Most e-mail programs keep a hidden copy of all e-mails you write and send, and e-mails can be forwarded without your permission, so don't write anything you wouldn't want the entire world to read. Finally, while an e-mail thank-you is better than none at all, it just won't do for special occasions.

Use e-mail for quick updates. E-mail is a good way to let people know what you're doing. It's quick and to the point. (Remember: e-mails should be brief; if you need to be more detailed, attach a document to your e-mail.)

Schedule regular briefings with your boss. Your boss doesn't need to know every detail of your day, but he or she might want a weekly update on where you are with your projects. In addition, if you can save all of your questions for the last ten minutes of the day, you might even improve your boss's productivity.

Schedule productive meetings with your colleagues. As we discussed in chapter 1, unfocused meetings can be huge time wasters. But if you and your colleagues are working on a project, a short but productive meeting can bring everyone up to date and will give you an opportunity to brainstorm solutions to obstacles that have popped up, as well as stay on top of any changes that have occurred.

Don't always be the one talking. Very few people really know how to listen effectively. But it's an extremely important skill to have if you're trying to improve communication. If you get a reputation as a good listener (which does require responding in the right places), you'll certainly hear more from your coworkers. (If this gets out of hand, however, check out some of my suggestions for avoiding time traps in chapter 1.)

Show some appreciation. If your coworkers come to you with a suggestion or idea, make sure they know you appreciate them and their hard work. If people feel good about themselves and the work they're doing, they'll be more open to what you're thinking and doing.

20 Really Useful Tip

Learn How to Deal with a Difficult Boss or Colleague

At my first job out of college, I worked for a guy who had a mouth like a sewer. While it was disturbing to hear him swear like Tony Soprano to customers and clients, it was far worse when he turned that attitude on me. After six months of verbal abuse, I couldn't take it anymore. I had turned into a quivering pot of jelly. So I quit.

After a few months of freelance writing, I took a job working for a woman who wouldn't look at me when we were having a conversation. Instead of looking at me, she looked away, out the window. (I later learned that she did this with many people, though not all.) When I first started working for her, I found the lack of eye contact to be disconcerting. Later on, it seemed downright rude, and by the end of our tenure together, I found it simply bizarre. The worst part about it? Her not looking at me while she was speaking to me made it a lot harder for me to read her body clues, figure out what was going on in her mind, and know what she wanted.

Of course, compared to Anne, I had it easy. She once worked for a guy who carried on rather amorous meetings with female coworkers. He asked Anne to cover for him when he was in one of these "closed-door sessions." One day, the CEO of her company came looking for her boss, who was in the middle of one of his "sessions." Anne told the CEO he was unavailable, and then shortly thereafter began looking for a new job.

Having a difficult boss is one of the biggest, and most pervasive, problems office workers face. While conducting research for this book, my staff and I interviewed more than a hundred workers at companies across the country. Almost all of them asked for help in dealing with a difficult boss or colleague.

One problem with suggesting ways to handle a difficult boss or colleague is that there are so many ways in which a boss or colleague can make life difficult. Your boss might be a micromanager, or he or she could be moody because of a personal crisis. Behavioral experts I spoke with offered a few simple pieces of advice for people who are dealing with a difficult boss or colleague:

The problem: You and your boss have communication problems. Perhaps you and your boss are on two different wavelengths. She takes everything you say the wrong way, and you feel that she isn't clear about what she wants and when she wants it. Your communication problems are causing friction, and you need to get the relationship back on track.

What should you do? Make a list of everything that bothers you about your relationship with your boss. Then pare that list down to its basic components. Schedule a meeting with your boss to go over the different issues that you have and propose solutions that might help ease the tension. Use these methods to help work things out with a difficult colleague as well.

The problem: You and your boss are motivated differently. Your boss's motivators are different from your own; perhaps he is motivated by a desire for recognition and you are motivated by a desire to accomplish goals. This incompatibility is putting a strain on your working relationship.

What should you do? Spend some time thinking about what motivates your boss. Understanding why your boss behaves the way he does will help you find some common ground on which to smooth over the tension. Although you and your boss may be motivated by different things at the office and in life, you can fine-tune the approach you take with your boss so that your work for him is more closely aligned with what he thinks you should do.

The problem: Your boss thinks you're making her look bad. Or your boss thinks you're not working hard enough to make her look good. This leads to her feeling suspicious about your actions and not entrusting certain projects to you.

What should you do? If you are deliberately making your boss look bad (a not-so-subtle form of office sabotage), it's a losing proposition all around: your boss looks bad, and in turn that casts a suspicious light on everyone who works for your boss as well. (If you're making your boss look bad in an attempt to get her removed from duty, it's unlikely that will happen without you getting fired as well.) If your boss just thinks you're trying to make her look bad, it may be because you're not trying to make her look good. If you make your boss look good, she will trust you more and will feel much better about your relationship. And there's always the chance that she will be promoted up and out.

The problem: Your boss's bad behavior continues. No matter what you do, your boss continues to act in a way that makes your office life miserable.

What should you do? Keep a log of issues that come up and your boss's response to them. If your boss leaves you an angry or abusive voice mail, consider taping it. If you are sent an inappropriate e-mail, you can print it and keep it in your file. If the difficulties continue, talk to your human resources department. If your company doesn't have a human resources department, speak to the office manager. If your boss is also the president of the company, or if you work at a family-owned business and you don't feel comfortable going to anyone for help, start looking for a new job. Life is too short to live under the strain of constant abuse.

The problem: Your boss is afraid to fail, so she micromanages everything. Your boss is so concerned about not failing that she watches over your shoulder, questions everything you do, and occasionally redoes what you've spent hours working on.

What should you do? By taking some initiative and showing your boss that you can get the work done, you might alleviate some of her fears, which should in turn ease the pressure. Stake a claim on a particular project and let your boss know what you're going to do—then do it. Take on as much as you can without going overboard, and then deliver.

The problem: Your boss tries to goad you into responding in a certain way. Your boss tries to bring you to his level by using abusive language or a condescending tone.

What should you do? No matter how bad it gets, don't stoop to his level. If you have a human resources department, ask them to help you transfer departments. If you don't, go to your office manager for help. If there's nowhere to go, start looking for a new job. At the end of the day, you have to live with yourself—which might be tough if you've done something you're not proud of.

Bonus Tip

If having a bad day turns into having a bad year, or having a bad lifetime, you may be dealing with someone who has bigger issues than a bad attitude. According to the Alexander Hamilton Institute (AHI), workplace bullying has turned into a serious issue. Apparently, all the schoolyard bullies grew up, but instead of growing out of their insecurities, they now take them out on their coworkers.

At AHI's Employment Law Resource Center (www.ahipubs.com), you can find tips on how to prevent workplace bullies from terrorizing everyone.

21 Really Useful Tip

Make Your Office Mates Feel Appreciated

"It's always worthwhile to make other people aware of their worth."

—Malcolm Forbes

When you walk into the lobby of WGN-TV, in Chicago, the first thing you see is a birthday and anniversary board. Each day, employees who are celebrating their birthday or anniversary of being employed by the station are listed. The board serves as a reminder to wish someone a happy birthday or congratulate someone during the day.

If you continue on toward the newsroom, you'll pass by the Employee of the Month board, which includes the photos and names of the winner in each month. Along with the prestige of winning, the employee of the month gets a terrific parking space for his or her monthlong reign.

Without spending a whole lot of cash, the station has found a way to say thank you to a few employees each day. And studies have shown that a simple thank-you not only makes employees feel appreciated, but also goes a long way toward building positive connections between employees and their clients and customers.

There are many good ways to say thank you, including by phone, in a note, or with a small token of your appreciation. (For years, I have been sending Frango Mints—a treat that used to be made in Chicago—to friends and colleagues.) But there are other ways to say thanks creatively while sticking to your budget.

Although there are no hard-and-fast rules about what types of occasions should receive special recognition, you should say congratulations or thank you if a colleague or boss (or, in some cases, a client or customer):

✓ Has a birthday
✓ Is celebrating an anniversary of employment, particularly a milestone anniversary (five, ten, or twenty years)
✓ Has delivered superior performance
✓ Has done you a favor
✓ Has given outstanding customer service
✓ Is retiring
✓ Has accepted a new job or promotion
✓ Has completed an important project
✓ Has opened a new office
✓ Is celebrating a personal milestone, such as a wedding or new baby

There are all sorts of ways to say thanks or congrats. For example, you can give:

✓ A certificate, plaque, or traveling trophy (which stays on the employee of the month's desk)
✓ A pen or desk accessory
✓ A watch or cool clock
✓ Tickets to a sporting or cultural event
✓ A gift certificate to a local restaurant
✓ A thank-you lunch for your coworkers at a local restaurant, or cookies and lemonade for an impromptu end-of-day celebration
✓ Extra time off
✓ An enhanced coffee break with donuts or a cake to recognize contributions

✓ A brag board (a bulletin board on which you recognize employee contributions by posting thank-you notes, memos, pictures, and other items)

✓ Cookies or chocolates (you can have a large thank-you cookie created at a local bakery)

✓ A donation to a favorite charity

Of course, simply saying thank you is a great way to make someone feel good about the extra effort or attention he or she has given something. With the advent of e-mail, the handwritten thank-you note has gone the way of the dodo bird. If you want to make someone feel great, put your thanks in writing. You may even want to make a copy and post it on the company brag board.

Saying Thanks to Your Boss

Most employees find it tough to say thanks to their boss without making it seem too personal. Since you don't want to send the wrong message, it's important to say thank you or congratulations in the right way. Depending on how well you know your boss, this can be quite a challenge.

When a line supervisor at a car company retired, his employees gave him a basket of grapefruit, a grapefruit knife, and a set of serrated spoons. A lover of grapefruit, he used the gift for years.

If you don't know your boss's taste personally, consider making something:

✓ Create a memory book and ask your coworkers to write their favorite work anecdotes of the preceding year. Include photos of company events.

✓ Create a "success board" documenting your boss's most successful projects.

✓ Take a photo of your work group, blow it up, and frame it.

✓ Make a cake or a basket of cookies (be sure to include an ingredients list in case your boss or someone in his or her family is allergic to a particular item, like peanuts).

Gift-Giving No-Nos

If you want to say thanks or congratulations and be taken seriously, take a wide path around these items:

✓   Gag gifts. They're never as funny as you think they are.

✓   Anything remotely sexual. This includes magazines, toys, or anything you'd feel funny showing your mother.

✓   Anything too personal. No frilly nightgowns, no special underwear, no perfume—nothing that might send the wrong message.

✓   Anything illegal.

22 Really Useful Tip

Polish Up on Cubicle Etiquette

Rock star Alice Cooper actually has an office. According to the *Wall Street Journal,* it's located in Phoenix, it's filled with show memorabilia, and it looks like it's decorated for Halloween year-round.

While decorating an office like this may work for a rock star, it's hardly appropriate in an office situation. Because people spend so much time in their offices or workspaces, how they look has an effect on how people work. In fact, we learned from the more than a hundred administrative assistants we surveyed that how you keep your cubicle or workspace can profoundly affect both mood and productivity. And since 90 percent of office workers sit in a cubicle rather than in a private office, cubicle etiquette is an issue high on everyone's hit list.

Although a cubicle is your personal workspace, you typically share common walls and airspace. Unless your cubicle has walls that go up to the ceiling, your neighbors can inadvertently eavesdrop on your most intimate conversations. Making your office a nicer place for everyone means paying attention to the fact that when you work in a cubicle environment, you're not working alone.

Here are some rules of cubicle etiquette that you'd be wise to follow if you want to get along with your coworkers and colleagues. If you have others you'd like to add to the list, e-mail me at ThinkGlink@aol.com.

The Ten Rules of Cubicle Etiquette

1. Be conscious of how loudly you speak. Don't say anything you don't want six other people to hear. (Your loud conversations might also distract or bother your coworkers.) A headset might help you speak more softly. If you have to have a personal conversation about something important, consider using a cell phone from outside the office or calling from an empty office or conference room.

2. Never use a speakerphone if you work in a cubicle. The only exception would be if you are in the office after hours and your office mates have gone home for the day.

3. Don't leave private mail, printed e-mails, bills, or legal documents out in the open. Anyone could see them. Keep these things locked up or put away if you're not at your desk. And don't read personal items that happen to be on your coworkers' desks.

4. Don't loiter around someone else's cubicle. Even if you've been invited over by a coworker, your presence could distract someone else. If you need to be there, pull over a chair and sit down.

5. Respect your coworkers' privacy. Don't look over their shoulders at their computers unless invited to do so.

6. If you want to play music, play it softly. Consider getting a headset that you can plug into your radio.

7. Don't smoke at your workspace. Although most companies now prohibit smoking indoors, a few don't. Keep in mind that smoke is absorbed by soft fabrics, including carpet, furniture upholstery, and window treatments.

8. Decorate carefully. Unless you work in a creative industry, like media or advertising, less is more here. A personal photo or two and perhaps a piece of art or a memento are about all you should have. And you should never have any photos, calendars, or other items of an obscene nature.

9. Watch for smells. If you eat at your desk, your food can produce unusual smells that can offend coworkers. If you need to eat at your desk and you've brought something particularly pungent for lunch, ask your surrounding coworkers if they mind the smell. (On the other hand, if you're making something appealing, offer to share.) The same is true about perfume. Many people are sensitive to strong fragrances. Although you may like wearing a particularly strong cologne, you're working in a shared environment. What smells good to you could give your coworker a headache.

10. Turn off your cell phone. Or put it on vibrate. Funny beeps and rings can annoy your colleagues.

TOP TIPS
for Running a Great Holiday Party

According to a survey by Hewitt Associates, an Illinois-based consulting company, only about a third of companies nation-wide were expected to give employees some type of holiday bonus in 2002. By contrast, two-thirds were expected to give a holiday party.

The problem with holiday parties is that most employees don't look forward to them. The days of excess wine and roses have faded away, and what's left just isn't that much fun.

The point of a holiday party is to help celebrate whatever holiday is at hand, to recognize the contributions of the office staff, and to boost morale. Here are some ways to liven up a holiday party:

Add a theme. In Britain, holiday parties are typically held with an "ugly" theme. In other words, you wear the ugliest tie, shirt, or headpiece you own. An editing firm in Chicago throws a holiday theme party every year and makes sure all of the details are in place. One year, they held a Turkish-themed party and used smoke makers to create a fake opium den.

Create a betting pool. Ask coworkers to join a betting pool for big events, such as the Super Bowl, the Oscars, or the World Series, or when a coworker will give birth. Keep the betting sheets, and at the holiday party reward the coworker who has placed the largest number of accurate bets. (No money need be involved.)

Take a photo. Bring a digital or Polaroid camera to the party and send partygoers home with funny photos.

Add some humor. Ask coworkers to bring in a funny cartoon or comic strip and add it to a humor board. You could also hold a joke-telling contest.

Have great, and unusual, food. Cheese cubes and crudités are hardly inspiring choices for a holiday party. It's much more fun to eat something unusual. Try Thai food or a ten-foot submarine sandwich (depending on how many people are attending the party). You could also offer a food group from each continent, or hold your party in an ethnic restaurant. If you're serving alcohol, offer drinks that are unusual as well. For example, if you're serving Japanese food, serve sake instead of wine.

Watch the clock. No matter how much fun your party is, most employees will just want to get home to be with their families. Limiting the festivities will make everyone enjoy the party that much more.

CHAPTER 5

*Making Your Office Safer
and More Comfortable*

How Your Office Environment Can Make Everyone Happier and More Productive

Take a minute and think about some of the most dangerous and uncomfortable places to work: deep in the recesses of a mine, or in the pit of an old steel mill, where temperatures easily reached over 125 degrees Fahrenheit.

While your life probably isn't at risk when you're at your desk typing away, studies have shown that the environment in which you work contributes to your good or ill health.

That's why office ergonomics has become such a hot topic. Ergonomics is the science of designing and arranging things that people use so that people interact with them more efficiently and safely. How you work in a space and the type of work you do both play a part in how good you feel going into the office day in and day out. (In fact, ergonomics has become such a hot button that in 2002, the U.S. Department of Labor's Occupational Safety and Health Administration [OSHA] announced the formation of the National Advisory Committee on Ergonomics.)

Take a typical doctor's office. Unless it's your child's pediatrician's office and it's been remodeled recently, most doctors' offices are quite bland. Behind the scenes, they're often disorganized, with papers and medical supplies everywhere. Patients often feel sick when they go to the doctor, but even if you go in for a checkup while you're well, you might not feel well afterward if your doctor's office isn't organized.

Recently, I visited the headquarters of the famed Rehabilitation Institute of Chicago. One of the doctors, Joel Press, and his staff teach people how to retrain their muscles to avoid aches and pains. Walking into the office, you see bright colors and a zippy design. From the curved welcome desk to the glass wall that allows light to come through, the office makes you feel better as soon as you walk through the door.

The latest thinking in office design is that an office should have a "sensory" or "holistic" layout. That is, the designer incorporates all five senses—sight, sound, taste, touch, and smell—and makes sure they work together to create a comfortable work environment:

Sight. Your office should be clutter free and have plenty of light (some sunlight is best, but proper lighting is essential), and it should include colors that are cheery but not busy. One brand-new real-estate office has celadon walls, cherry furniture, and huge, inexpensive, and colorful glass vases that are lit beautifully with small halogen lights, making it an environment that is calm and appealing.

Sound. Some people get annoyed with constant music in the background, but a constant sound can help to soothe your senses. If the office buzz or your office mates' conversations are making you crazy, try creating some white noise with a desktop waterfall.

Touch. Touching is a way for us to make connections with the outside world. In an office, each surface should be as pleasant to touch as possible—and be clean as well. When Jackie, a producer for a news show, starts her shift, she first takes a napkin and wipes down her desk and keyboard (which she shares with other producers) with hydrogen peroxide. She says it not only helps kill the germs that come from dozens of people touching the same keyboard every day, but it also keeps her healthy during the winter.

Smell. Real-estate agents often say that if you want to sell your home, bake some bread. (In other books I've written, I suggest getting a roll of cookie dough from your refrigerated section and baking it on tinfoil just before a showing.) Making your home smell good helps awaken a prospective buyer's sense of longing. The same is true in an office. Good smells make us feel happier. While you typically can't bake cookies in an office, you can brew fresh coffee. Or you can bring in some fresh flowers or plug in an air freshener. And again, cleanliness is important: no smell is preferable to a bad one.

Taste. Often, food is omnipresent in offices. Many employees eat at their desks. Some offices have cafeterias, and others bring in food once a week as a thank-you for their employees. Having food at a workplace can make it feel homier. The Leo Burnett advertising agency has a big bowl of fresh apples next to the receptionist's desk. The Irving B. Harris Foundation, a nonprofit specializing in early childhood development, keeps an office kitchen stocked with juices, fruit, snacks, and candy. At Bloomberg Financial, in New York, a similar assortment is set out in the hallway between everyone's offices. That way, if you don't want to leave work, you don't have to.

Your office or workspace should also reflect your personality. Roger is a frequent flier. Because he likes (or has grown used to) sitting in airplane seats, he put a pair of commercial airline seats in a separate area next to his office. He says it helps him do some of his best thinking. "It's important to have places where people can get away from their everyday work responsibilities," Roger told the *Wall Street Journal.*

Making your office a place where everyone likes to be will make your coworkers and colleagues happier and more productive. It doesn't have to be expensive, and it doesn't have to take a long time.

Incremental changes can work wonders.

23 Really Useful Tip

Choose and Use the Right Equipment and Furniture for Your Office

"The fingers of a typist may exert up to 25 tons of force every day."
—U.S. Department of Labor

Sit in a bad chair for three hours straight every day, without moving, and you're bound to end up with bad back. But it doesn't have to be that way. Two studies completed in the 1980s showed that worker productivity increased 25 percent when offices were modified to be more ergonomic.

You don't have to petition management to buy all new furniture. You can modify what you have or learn how to better use what you have if you can't afford the trendiest office furniture on the market.

Chairs

If you sit in a chair for several hours a day, you should try to find one that won't inhibit the circulation in your legs or make your back stiff. Any old chair will do if you're in your early twenties (ah, youth!), but as we age, things like poor circulation and back problems make an ergonomic chair essential. And

Quill has a staff of furniture specialists who can help you design your office. They'll draw up a floor plan, send you samples, and help you choose furniture that meets your ergonomic requirements. They'll even come out to your office if you need extra help. See Quill.com for details, or call 800-634-0321.

although young bodies can endure uncomfortable chairs, they may lead to problems down the line, or sooner than they would appear if you were using a better chair.

According to Grace Walker, a registered physical therapist and occupational therapist in Texas, the most common problems her patients have stem from chairs and desks. She says that office chairs are usually too short, don't have a lever to raise or lower them automatically, and put a lot of strain on the lower back. Desks are typically positioned at the wrong angle for the arms. If you're seated in the right place, the desk should be at a ninety-degree angle to your hands and arms.

A properly designed and adjusted chair will provide support to the back, legs, buttocks, and arms. This support can reduce contact stress, overexertion, and fatigue and will promote proper circulation in your legs and arms.

The seat should be contoured, and you should be able to adjust the height of the chair. How high should you place the chair? According to the Department of Labor, the chair height is correct when the entire sole of the foot can rest on the floor or a footrest and when the back of the knee is slightly higher than the seat of the chair. This position allows blood to circulate freely in the legs and feet. Some chair designers say your legs should be at least at a ninety-degree angle to your desk.

Armrests are often too high or too low, which can be awkward and uncomfortable. Adjustable armrests can help provide the correct support.

While some ergonomic chairs are expensive (a thousand dollars or more), a fairly good chair can be had for a few hundred dollars. If you can't get your boss to pay for a new chair, it might be worth investing in one just to save your neck, back, arms, and legs. If you don't know what a good, ergonomic chair looks like, check out the supply at Quill.com.

If the odds of getting your boss to buy you a new chair are next to nil, you can inexpensively improve the lumbar support you're getting by using back cushions, backrests, or Polartec back perches. Quill.com offers dozens of inexpensive ways to improve the chair you already have. If your feet dangle instead of sitting firmly on the floor, your desk may be too tall for you. An ergonomically correct, adjustable footrest can solve this problem.

Desks

If your chair height can be adjusted, the type of desk you have isn't that important. The main objective is that it is deep enough to give you enough distance (a minimum of twenty-five inches) from your computer monitor.

Another important factor is how you have your stuff arranged on your desk. Everything should be within easy reach, including your keyboard, mouse, telephone, Palm, and notepad. You shouldn't have to strain or twist to reach anything, including your files. If you have file cabinets located beneath your desk, make sure you can reach them easily.

Make sure your desk gives you enough room between your knees and the desktop. You should have about three inches, or enough to comfortably cross your legs.

Sometimes, the solution is so easy it's overlooked. Have you ever had a wobbly table in a restaurant? The waiter probably fixed it by stuffing a matchbox under the short leg. If your desk is slightly too low, consider raising it an inch or so by using a small piece of plywood or a rubber disk under each leg. Ask your maintenance department if they have something that might work, or choose from a variety of fix-it solutions at your local home improvement store.

Desk organizers can help as long as you use them. There are different types of organizers, including wire or wood separators that keep your pencils separate from your paper clips in your desk drawer. Or try an organizer that sits on top of your desk.

If you spend hours on the telephone every day, you could be straining your neck, particularly if you try to type while you're cradling the phone between your ear and shoulder. Telephone headsets are inexpensive and allow you to keep your head straight while talking and typing.

File Cabinets
It's too easy to pull your back muscles trying to open a sticky file cabinet. Make sure your cabinets and drawers open easily. If they don't, see if you can use a lubricant to make them easier to use.

Computers and Monitors
In the world of computers, monitors are getting larger, and we're sitting closer to them. While having a larger monitor can be a

It's important not to overload a file cabinet. If your file cabinet gets stuffed, it will be much more difficult to open and could break. Instead of over-stuffing, purchase a few extra plastic or cardboard filing boxes and store away the unused or older parts of your files.

Quill
suggests

good thing, a monitor that's too close to (or too far from) your eyes is never a good thing.

Ergonomic experts say the eyes-to-screen distance should be at least twenty-five inches. You can either measure this with a ruler or simply take your arm and hold it out. The monitor shouldn't be any closer than the end of your arm (unless you have really long arms). If you can't read the letters, you should either increase the pitch size on your computer or get your glasses adjusted.

When looking at a computer, you should ideally look down at the screen. This doesn't have to be dramatic. While some

Have you ever looked through a dirty camera lens? The dust, water spots, and particles can ruin your pictures. In the same way, a dirty monitor can ruin your eyes. Most of us never clean our monitor screens, and our eyes can be strained by struggling to look through the dirt to our work on the screen. Clean your monitor regularly with a screen cleaner that will safely remove dust and fingerprints from the screen while adding a layer of static protection.

Quill
suggests

Quill's technology specialists can help you choose the right computer hardware and software for your business. Contact them through Quill.com or call 800-789-0041.

Quill
suggests

offices put monitors into specially built desks with glass tops, you can simply tilt the top of your monitor so it is slightly farther from the eyes than the bottom of the monitor is. This helps prevent glare, which can also strain your eyes. If you have a choice of screen colors, choose dark letters on a light background.

In many ways, having a window next to your desk or behind you is lucky, but one downside is that your monitor may appear to function as a mirror rather than as something connected to a computer. Use screen filters to dampen glare and enhance resolution. Filters can also help keep your work private, as anyone not seated in your chair would have a hard time seeing what's on your screen.

If you have to read while you're typing, it helps to have a copyholder, or plastic arm, attached to the side of your computer. It holds your documents, allowing you to keep your neck and head straight while typing.

With all of the computer equipment in offices these days, we often trip up on cords and cables. You might want to use plastic ties or even plastic tubing to hold cords in place and keep them together.

Keypads and Wrist Rests

Keypads and wrist rests are an important part of workspace ergonomics. If you don't have your elbows, wrists, and hands positioned correctly, you could end up with a host of problems, including carpal tunnel syndrome (CTS) (numbness, swelling,

Keyboard trays that attach just below your desk allow you to rest your arm on your chair armrests and keep your hands in the correct position. If you're tight on desk space, keyboard trays can free some up. A soft, raised wrist rest will help keep your wrists and hands straight when you're typing.

and pain in the hands and wrists), rotator injuries (particularly after age forty), and neck and shoulder pain.

Ergonomics experts say you need to get your elbows off the desk and allow your hands to type freely. (You should also take frequent breaks. See chapter 7 for hand-stretching exercises.)

Your Mouse

It's easy to overstretch to reach your mouse. But you have to fight that temptation and instead position your mouse so that it is right next to your keyboard.

If you do a lot of clicking, you may want to look into a mouse that allows you to click with a different finger or one that better fits the shape of your hand. People with larger hands, for example, might be more comfortable using a larger mouse. That's what Dr. Alan Hedge, a Cornell professor of ergonomics, found in a 1999 study that compared how people responded in two-minute sessions to a basic mouse and one called "The Whale."

If the mouse that came with your computer doesn't work for you, check out alternative sizes and shapes. Visit a local computer store and play with the different mouse options, or go online to Quill.com to see some of the latest innovations in mouse design.

If you notice that your desktop and monitor are dusty week in and week out, or that dust quickly settles even after you've just wiped everything down, it could be that the air quality in your office is poor. Consider investing in a small air cleaner and keeping it below or next to your desk. If the dust is settling on your desk and monitor, you're probably breathing it in as well.

24 Really Useful Tip

Shed a Little Light on the Subject

If basic office fluorescent lighting hurts your eyes, you may want to make some adjustments to bring the softer lighting of home into your workspace. The idea is to eliminate harsh contrasts and glare than can strain your eyes. Tabletop, halogen, or task lighting can make it easier to see what you're doing.

Let's start with some lighting basics:

Flood lights light a large space from above.

Task lights throw a directed beam onto a particular part of your workspace.

Ambient lights spread light out or bounce it off of walls or the ceiling.

Natural light is provided by windows, although halogen lights closely mirror its color and feel.

Natural light is the best, although direct sunlight can intensify the glare on your monitor, and the fading light of sunset can decrease your ability to see. So even if you are lucky enough to sit by a window, you'll need additional sources of light to do your best work.

You'll also need additional light if you're over thirty. According to several studies, including a 1995 study sponsored by the Lighting Research Institute, the older we are, the more light we need to do the same tasks. In fact, if you're over the age of seventy, glare affects your vision twice as much as it does when you're in your fifties. Adding a table lamp or under-counter halogen lights to your workspace may dramatically increase your productivity. You'll also need additional light if you're reading small print or doing fine motor work, like changing the battery on a wristwatch.

Warmer light (provided by incandescent or halogen bulbs) mixed with cooler light (provided by fluorescent bulbs) can help you feel better in your workplace. Studies have shown that exposure to bright lights on winter days can help improve people's mood and temperament. Check out different lighting options at Quill.com or call 800-789-1331 for the complete lighting catalog.

Adjusting the Light in Your Workspace

Here are a few pointers to keep in mind when adjusting the light in and around your workspace:

✓ Place your computer at a ninety-degree angle to a window to minimize glare.

✓ If you can move your desk, try to position your chair so that it is between overhead fluorescent fixtures.

✓ If you sit next to or facing a window that gets direct sunlight during part or all of the day, purchase window blinds that can temper the strength of the direct light. Or use a glare screen.

✓ Place task lighting to the right of your right hand (if you're right-handed) or to the left of your left hand (if you're left-handed). This should eliminate shadows on your work papers.

✓ If you need more general lighting, try an inexpensive, freestanding halogen torch lamp (but keep it away from curtains and other flammable objects).

Quiz

Do You Have an Ergonomic Problem in Your Office?

More than a hundred different injuries can be caused by ergonomic problems in the office. Take this quiz to see if there are places where you need to make adjustments.

☐ Do you feel stressed while doing your job?

☐ Do you feel tired while working?

☐ Do you rub your eyes? Do you feel like you're straining your eyes to see your computer monitor or the work on your desk?

☐ Do you get frequent headaches while working?

☐ Do you feel like your glasses prescription isn't strong enough? Do you experience blurry vision?

☐ Have you developed back problems since starting this job? Does your back hurt constantly while you're at your desk?

☐ Have you developed neck problems since starting this job?

☐ Do your hands or wrists hurt or tingle while typing for long periods of time?

☐ Do you have to turn your head to see your computer monitor?

☐ Do your feet touch the floor when you're sitting at your desk?

☐ Does the light in your office hurt your eyes? Or does it seem too dark in your office?

☐ Do you have to look up to see your computer monitor?

☐ Do you hunch your shoulders or neck while holding the phone or doing other things?

☐ Do you unconsciously raise your shoulders while typing?

If you answered yes to any of these questions, see the specific sections in this chapter that apply to your problems, or visit the sites below.

For More Information

For more information on ergonomics, check out Cornell University's Ergonomics Web site (http://ergo.human.cornell.edu) or the U.S. Department of Labor (www.dol.gov).

Quill's furniture specialists can offer insight on the right lights for your office. Go to Quill.com or call 800-634-0321 for details.

For More Information

Check out the American Lighting Association's Web site (www.americanlightingassoc.com) or the U.S. Department of Labor's Web site (www.dol.gov).

25 Really Useful Tip

Improve Office Safety and Security

"Homicide is the second leading cause of death in the workplace. The first is work-related injuries."
—OSHA

You can worry all you like about a coworker or colleague "going postal," but you're much more likely to slip, trip, or fall in your office. In a recent study by the Ohio Industrial Commission, slips, trips, and falls accounted for 64 percent of all office injuries.

Most of these could have been prevented, which is why office safety is an important enough topic to warrant its own book. (And many have been written.) But by taking a little extra care and taking a few of the following suggestions, you'll have the ability to make your office a safer and more secure place to spend a third or more of your day.

There are six causes of office injuries:
- ✓ Slips, trips, and falls
- ✓ Improperly used or faulty equipment
- ✓ Collisions or obstructions
- ✓ Falling objects or being caught between objects
- ✓ Fire and electricity
- ✓ Miscellaneous, including horseplay and accidents that don't fit anywhere else

Being aware of common hazards is half the battle, says Brian Preston, Quill's head of security. The Division of Safety and Hygiene of the Ohio Industrial Commission suggests office workers watch out for these potentially hazardous conditions:

✓ Poorly lit floors, including in storage areas where boxes and other materials are left scattered around

✓ Spills, particularly on a hard surface

✓ Bad weather days, and coworkers and colleagues who track in mud, snow, rain, and salt

✓ Slippery, poorly marked, blocked or clogged stairways

✓ Damaged floor surfaces, including carpet that is unraveling

✓ Highly polished or uneven floors

✓ Poor workspace layout, including desks with drawers that open into walkways and unseen filing cabinets that open unexpectedly into aisles

✓ Open drawers or cabinets that do not latch properly

✓ Telephone, computer, and other electrical cords that are not well-organized or grouped together or are frayed

✓ Poorly maintained electrical equipment, including coffeemakers, copiers, pencil sharpeners, and space heaters, and overloaded electrical outlets

✓ Rough edges, chips, or burs on furniture that can snag clothes or cause cuts and bruises

✓ Poorly stacked books, papers, or files

✓ Cabinets that are top-heavy

✓ Chairs that tilt too far back or are used as impromptu ladders

Since slips, trips, and falls account for the bulk of office accidents, here are a few suggestions from the Atlanta-based Office of Health and Safety, Centers for Disease Control and Prevention (CDC), on what you can do to help make your office a safer place to work:

✓ Make sure the hallway or path is clear before you walk.

✓ Close drawers completely after using them.

✓ Avoid excessive bending, twisting, and leaning backward while seated.

✓ Secure electrical cords and wires away from walkways and from where your feet are under your desk.

✓ Always use a stepladder (not a chair) for reaching objects.

✓ Clean up spills immediately or call someone if you don't know what the liquid is.

✓ Pick up objects left on the floor or move them to the side.

✓ Call building security if you see a loose tile, unraveling carpet, or damaged flooring.

✓ Never carry anything that obscures your vision.

✓ Wear stable shoes with nonslip soles.

Poor Indoor Air Quality

Today's offices contain new hazards brought on by the increased use of technology and different methods of building design. In addition to the more common hazards of a slippery floor, an unraveling rug, or an open file cabinet, these other concerns include poor lighting, noise, poorly designed furniture, and equipment and machines that emit gases and vapors even when properly maintained.

Indoor air quality is a hot topic amongst safety engineers, as people become more sensitive to odd odors and as new, fully sealed buildings make the problem more difficult to spot. According to the Office of Health and Safety, odors might come from chemicals inside or outside an office space, or even from the construction of a building. Some likely suspects include building renovations, new carpet, paints, adhesives, sealants, office furniture (particularly pieces made from non-natural materials), or vinyl wall coverings.

But poor air quality can be caused by a badly designed ventilation system. So inside your office you might be smelling and breathing in things from the outside, including pollen, dust, and mold spores, car and truck exhaust, and even odors from dumpsters.

If your office smells funny, you can try a personal air filter. If that doesn't work, talk to the building manager or the coworker who is in charge of office safety about whether other steps could be taken to make sure the air in your office is safe to breathe.

Preparing Your Office for an Emergency

A few years ago, my husband, Sam, was walking through Sam's Club when he spotted a first-aid kit. It was the size of a small briefcase, and it claimed to contain almost everything you'd ever need. He bought two, and we've kept them in our home since. They've come in very handy when someone gets hurt (as little children often do).

Sam's brother, Mitch, worked in the first World Trade Center building hit in the terrorist attacks of September 11. His office was on the seventy-eighth floor, and it was the only office on that floor that had a first-aid kit. Mitch's employees were so busy bandaging the wounded that they were among the last people to get out of the building before it collapsed.

You never know when you'll be faced with an emergency. Remember that an ounce of prevention is worth a pound of care. Here are some suggestions for preparing your office for any emergency:

Develop an evacuation plan. Your office should practice evacuating. Time your evacuation so you know how effective your plan is. Decide where to meet once you're out of the building so you can quickly figure out if everyone is accounted for.

Know where emergency exits are. It's important to make sure the exits really open and are not blocked by heavy boxes or other items that could delay your departure.

Keep a list of emergency numbers handy. This includes internal office extensions as well as the numbers for local police and fire stations (this will often be "911") and the center for poison control.

Know where the closest fire extinguisher is. Make sure it isn't so old that it would be useless in an emergency. And know how to use it so you don't end up spraying yourself or someone else in the eyes.

Know where the first-aid kit is. Be sure it contains enough bandages, disinfectant, and aspirin (or ibuprofen) to take care of injuries caused by slips, trips, and falls. If your company doesn't have a first-aid kit, ask your office manager or boss to purchase one. Or offer to purchase it yourself and have the company reimburse you.

Keep eyewash handy, particularly if your office is dusty. You can find a wide selection of first-aid and emergency solutions at Quill.com.

Office Security

Although we may think we know our coworkers and colleagues, crime still happens in office environments. And in today's high-tech world, it isn't just money that gets taken. Identity theft is a growing problem, and many offices contain highly sensitive information not only about their employees but about their customers as well.

In fact, security breaches cost American businesses more than two billion dollars a year in missed sales and wasted research and development. One-third of all workers steal from their employers, costing an estimated loss of five to ten billion dollars. Employee theft is one of the top reasons small businesses fail. And a coworker experiencing severe financial difficulties is more likely to steal from a colleague or the business, according to John Waskin, an author and consultant on financial matters.

If a couple has seventy thousand dollars in credit card debt, most of it charged by one spouse, "imagine the [other spouse's] pressure at work every day. Debt relates to our work ethic," Waskin explained. "No one wants people working in their accounting department if they're having money troubles."

According to a study by Virginia Tech University and to facts reported by the National Council on Economic Education:

- ✓ Two-thirds of employees say they have had trouble paying their bills on time and worry about money.
- ✓ Seventy-five percent of employees say they have recently faced at least one significant financial problem.
- ✓ More than a third of the workforce says money worries sometimes hamper job performance.
- ✓ Fifteen percent of employees in the U.S. are so stressed financially that their job is negatively impacted. More than 20 percent of our armed forces say they are stressed financially.
- ✓ Of those employees who have credit card debt and are late paying, more than 33 percent waste twenty-one work hours a month dealing with money matters, according to Waskin.

For More Information

If you're having money troubles, they're not going to go away without some effort on your part. Check out John Waskin's Web site (www.billfree.org), the National Foundation for Credit Counseling's Consumer Credit Counseling Services (www.nfcc.org), and the Federal Trade Commission's site (www.ftc.gov), each of which provides detailed information on saving money and managing debt.

TOP TIPS
for Preventing Crime in Your Office

Here are some precautions you can take to prevent a crime from occurring in your office:

- ✓ Lock your door, filing cabinets, and desk when you leave, even if you're just leaving for lunch.
- ✓ If you're in charge of personnel files or other sensitive information, make sure this information is locked up twenty-four hours a day.
- ✓ Keep your purse or wallet, cell phone, and other personal belongings in a safe place during the day.
- ✓ Create computer passwords that include numbers and letters. Change them often.
- ✓ Don't write down passwords and safe combinations. Commit these to memory.
- ✓ Do not remove rings, watches, bracelets, or other jewelry when washing your hands.
- ✓ Keep information about equipment that you have purchased, including the amount you spent, when you bought it, and the serial numbers.
- ✓ Frequently back up your computer hard drive and keep the copy locked up in a secure location.

There are different types of equipment that will help keep your office safe. Cross shredders are a must for keeping sensitive papers out of the wrong hands. Desk-drawer safes can be bolted into the drawer and then locked with a key or keypad punch. Security cabinets can be bolted to the wall and locked. Fireproof, waterproof file chests can lock away sensitive files, CDs, Zip disks, and other information.

CHAPTER 6

Using Technology to Make It Easy

How Ten Years of Innovation Has Revolutionized What We Do and How We Do It

A decade ago, the Internet was just beginning to make a buzz. I was getting ready to ship my first book, *100 Questions Every First-Time Home Buyer Should Ask,* off to the publisher, and my editor asked if I'd like to include an e-mail address so that readers could reach me. The last thing I did before heading out to the post office was sign up for America Online (which at the time had maybe a million subscribers—if that many) and get my first e-mail account.

Today, it's almost hard to imagine life without e-mail and the Internet. In less than ten years, this little bit of hardware and code has completely changed the way we communicate with one another and do business. It has created new industries and sunk others. It has made billionaires of high school and college dropouts and has bankrupted those who bet the wrong way. It has brought to your desktop more information than you could ever find at the best public library in town, and it has made this information accessible 24/7/365.

If you think about the introduction of the transistor, the television tube, and Henry Ford's car, you start to see that the first ten or even twenty years of a revolution are nothing compared to what we do with it fifty or a hundred years later. If a hundred years after the first affordable car rolled off the assembly lines we're introducing übercars that cost $350,000 to $750,000, you have to wonder what we'll be doing with the Internet in another ninety years.

Technology will be with us for our lifetimes. And it will continually change how we do things. Our children will never know life without computers, Touch-Tone phones, cell phones, or calculators. They will grow up keeping their calendars online, communicating with one another by e-mail, and wondering what "records" are. They will think nothing of banking online, paying bills online, and buying things online.

Technology can make our lives easier—if we let it.

26 Really Useful Tip

Upgrade Office Efficiency with Computers, Laptops, and Networks

In 1988, I bought my first computer. I had just started out my career as a freelance writer and needed something on which to write my stories. The computer was made by Hyundai (I used to joke that the assembly line alternated between cars and computers), and it had an amber screen and a 640K memory. It cost eighteen hundred dollars, and was hands down the best investment I ever made in my company.

Over the next fifteen years, I purchased at least eight or nine additional computers, including two laptops. In the early years, I upgraded my computers about every three years. Lately, it seems as though we buy a computer every year. For the same $1,800 (or as little as $499), we can get thousands of times the computing power, all kinds of bells and whistles, and even an addictive game called Spider Solitaire.

Although it feels expensive while you're paying the bill, upgrading your technology can make your company much more productive.

Michael, a senior vice president in charge of sales for a start-up company, says he can travel the world with three things: his laptop, cell phone, and Palm. That's all he needs to conduct business. Gerhard, an international business consultant, agrees, though he will sometimes bring along a portable printer if he has to do presentations in remote locations.

Will upgrading your technology improve your office efficiency? If you haven't bought a new system in the past three to five years, the answer is almost certainly.

Selling Your Vision

Upgrading your office technology takes a few skills you may not have used before:

Vision. The computing possibilities are endless—if only you can imagine them. Upgrading your system should give you the ability to eliminate redundant tasks, enhance intra- and interoffice communication, and immediately access information you need to do your job. The technology you buy should also allow you to upgrade your software, improve record keeping, and design graphically enhanced sales tools, proposals, and presentations. At several major television stations, upgrading technology meant taking a huge leap from a linear editing system that was slow and cumbersome to a digital, computer-based system that is lean and fast.

Research. Once you have the vision, you have to figure out what kinds of components will deliver the results you want. Do you need a new desktop network? Or will several individual systems accomplish the task? Does your system need to be portable? Perhaps you need to add a few laptops to the mix. Do you need to upgrade the server on your Web site? Do you need color printers with additional memory to print the newly graphic presentations once you've created them? The nice thing about buying technology today is that you can customize your system and buy only the pieces you need. Think about what else has to be done to accommodate your vision: new furniture, wiring, upgraded Internet access, better security, additional training. Itemize all of these costs and determine how long it will take to implement the plan.

Sales. If you want to upgrade technology, you'll have to sell your boss or the office manager on your vision. Your boss will be interested in how it can help, but he or she will be really interested in how much you can save in terms of time and money. For example, if upgrading your system will allow the office accounting program to stop crashing (saving you hours of time reentering data), it's probably an easy sell. If upgrading means you can produce fabulous sales brochures in-house instead of using an outside graphic designer or ad agency, you will probably get the okay.

Compromise. It's possible that your technology proposal will be accepted on the spot. More likely, you'll have to compromise on some features and expenses, or if it's a big expense, you may have to spread out the costs over a year.

Do You Need a Network?

Networking your system means information will flow more freely between coworkers and colleagues. (It does not necessarily mean that your employer will be spying on you, although that will certainly be easier to do on a network than on an individual system.)

Allowing information, files, notes, case histories, presentations, and sales kits to be available at the click of a button should make your office much more productive. Dwight, a former computer consultant turned commercial developer, has just three computers in his office. Yet he has networked them so that everyone has access to the same information no matter which computer station he or she is logged into, thus saving his staff time and energy—which translates into money saved for the company.

Sally, a secretary in a small law firm, has seen the benefits of networking firsthand. If her boss needs to create a new legal document, she can log on to the firm's electronic library to see if another lawyer or secretary has already created a similar document. She and her boss will save time (and their client's money) if they can modify a colleague's existing document rather than creating one from scratch.

If you have offices in several locations—even within the same building—you'll probably want to create a network. Your network could make use of the Internet or include a private Intranet that can be accessed only by employees.

When it comes to upgrading your system, you may not need to throw out what you have. Simply upgrading certain features could give you the boost you're looking for. At Quill.com, you'll find cameras, scanners, computer accessories, data-storage drives and media, handheld computers, software, and other items that can upgrade your system quickly.

Bonus Tip

Although ATM machines allow you to easily access your bank accounts from anywhere in the world (and take out cash for a small fee or for free within your own network), according to one banking survey about 10 percent of the population doesn't trust them and never will. Some people are afraid of technology. Others fear change itself. Even if upgrading your office computers will make life easier and more productive for everyone, at least one individual is sure to balk at the idea and try to throw a wrench into your plans. So here's a tip to help make it easier all around: before you try to sell your plan to management, be sure to spend some time selling it to your colleagues and coworkers. Be ready to hold someone's hand through the process or provide a psychological boost to those who welcome change but are afraid they won't be able to master the technology.

For More Information

The major hardware manufacturers include Dell (Dell.com), IBM (IBM.com), Compaq (Compaq.com), Gateway (Gateway.com), and Apple (Apple.com). Each of these companies offers extensive information about a wide variety of products on their Web sites. You can play around with different features and see how different configurations change the price of an individual computer or laptop. If you are buying a number of machines, you should decide which company you want to work with and find someone there who can help you set up the system you want with the features you need.

27 Really Useful Tip

Make Use of Cell Phones, Pagers, Wireless Handhelds, and Other Handheld Devices

April works for a large financial company with offices in New York, Chicago, and London. Her boss is on the road 50 percent of the time, and April says that if it wasn't for his cell phone and pager, she'd never be able to find him.

Remember the days when you had to search around to find a pay phone? Or had to pay exorbitant rates from a hotel because there were no pay phones around?

Those days are over. In the past fifteen years, cell phones have morphed from large, awkward objects that were outrageously expensive to buy and use to slim, trim devices that allow you to make long-distance calls less expensively than you can with your landline at home (if you get the right package and don't go over your allotted minutes each month).

And everyone seems to have them—kids, moms, dads, grandparents, babysitters. Certainly, they are de rigueur for the busy executive, but they have become so affordable and necessary that just about everyone else has them too. If your boss doesn't have a cell phone, and you have trouble getting in touch with him when he is on the road, check your local paper for the deals of the day. (Cell phone companies tend to advertise often.)

If your boss doesn't like the idea of a cell phone, perhaps he or she will agree to get a pager. A pager is a small device that you can either wear on your belt or put in your purse. It allows people all over the world to let you know they'd like to talk to you. The caller can also leave you a text message or a phone number so you can return the call.

A Cell Phone for You

If your boss frequently sends you out on errands or has you handle business for the company outside the office, ask her if you should get a cell phone or a pager that the company would pay for. This way, your boss can be in constant contact with you.

The Next Generation

Today's pagers are sort of old school compared with the next generation of handheld devices that incorporate multiple functions. Typically, you get a wireless e-mail system combined with a pager and perhaps a telephone.

A BlackBerry, for example, can act as a pager, but it is a wireless minicomputer that allows you to access your e-mail and write or respond to messages. The latest generation includes a telephone, so you can also talk to the office. Tracking software has been developed that allows you to find the location of a particular BlackBerry (and hopefully the boss or colleague who is

If you're looking for an all-in-one device, be sure it has all the capabilities (cell phone, wireless e-mail, instant messenger, ordinary writing system—not the Palm writing—and tiny computer keyboard) included in a slick-looking package. The companies to watch include BlackBerry, Handspring, Palm, and Motorola. Visit Quill.com for the most current versions.

Quill suggests

carrying it). And if a BlackBerry is stolen, software at the office can "lock down" the device remotely, preventing sensitive information from disappearing or being read by the wrong individual.

Palm has created a number of handheld devices that allow you to manage your calendar, access an electronic address book, and take notes in a meeting. The Palm "docks" in a small port that is attached to your computer. You can upload information from your Palm to the computer home program or download information to your Palm.

Bonus Tip

If you don't have a cell phone, or if you are traveling to Europe, Asia, or Latin America where your cell phone won't work, consider using a prepaid phone card. You can purchase prepaid phone cards just about everywhere, from corner grocery stores to gas stations. But the "cleanest cards," that is, the cheapest cards with the least fees, are available from Sam's Club and Costco, and you can buy and recharge the Costco card online.

28 Really Useful Tip

Understand the Differences between DSL, Cable Modems, ISDN, and T-1 Lines

There are two things to know about connecting to the Internet. The first is that the faster you go, the more it's going to cost. The second is that even the most reliable technology sometimes fails.

But you have to start somewhere. Here is a basic guide to the different types of connectivity that are currently available, along with a rough estimate of pricing:

DSL

DSL stands for Digital Subscriber Line. Generally speaking, it is distance sensitive, which means that the closer you are to the telephone company's central office, the faster your service will be. If you are far away from the central office, your DSL will work like a regular modem.

There are three forms of DSL:

ADSL

Residential users get ADSL (Asymmetric Digital Subscriber Line). This typically offers a "downstream" speed that is twice as fast as the "upstream" speed. In other words, you can download

Web pages or videos at a high speed, but any information you send will travel at a significantly slower speed.

$ Cost: Less than $70 per month plus installation

SOHO

Small to medium-sized businesses can try SOHO (Small Office Home Office), which is a step up in terms of speed and line quality from ADSL and is designed for use by a three-person office.

$ Cost: Less than $150 per month plus installation

SDSL

The top quality DSL is called SDSL (Symmetric Digital Subscriber Line). Unlike ADSL, with its different upload and download speeds, you get the same high speed when you're sending and receiving, and the line quality is very stable. The speed is similar to that of a T-1 line.

$ Cost: Varies, but expect to pay more than $200 per month

Digital Cable Modems

A digital cable modem is an option for very small offices (one to two employees) or even a home office. It uses the same cable wire that you use to receive cable television and can match the speed of both DSL and T-1 technology. However, if too many people (either in your office or down the road) are using the cable wire at the same time, the speed and line quality degrade. It is not really a good solution for an office of significant size.

$ Cost: Similar to DSL, less than $70 per month

ISDN

ISDN (Integrated Services Digital Network) is a special, certified telephone line that provides speeds of up to 128 Kbps, which is slower than DSL. However, two ISDN lines can be bonded together to upgrade the speed. ISDN lines are also able to transmit studio-quality voice lines, so depending on your needs, this may be a good choice.

Unfortunately, it only works reliably for small businesses in urban environments. Offices in rural locations may find the service spotty. Bad weather can affect usability as well.

$ Cost: Less than $100 per month plus installation

T-1 and T-3 Lines

If you need the fastest, securest link to the Internet or for transmission, you'll want to use a T-1 or T-3 line.

A T-1 line runs at a reliable 1.5 Mbps, which is about twenty-eight times as fast as a typical dial-up modem or leased line. A T-1 line is dependable and secure because the special telephone line it uses runs in an unbroken connection between two points. It is ideal for larger offices because hundreds of users can access a T-1 line at the same time and enjoy the top rate of speed. Unfortunately, it is not available in all locations.

If you think a T-1 line is fast, try a T-3. A T-3 line runs three times as fast as a T-1, and thousands of users can access it simultaneously.

$ Cost: For a T-1 line, expect to spend up to $600 per month plus installation; for a dedicated T-3 circuit, the cost will be several times as much

If you're trying to meet the needs of a large office, talk to a telecomm specialist who can help you find the best deal available in your area. Quill's technology specialists may also be able to help you figure out what kind of hardware you need to run your office. Contact them through Quill.com or call 800-789-0041.

For More Information

Check out the Broadband Reports Web site FAQs page at www.dslreports.com/faq.

29 Really Useful Tip

Make Teleconferencing and Videoconferencing Work for You

A decade ago, I wrote a story about the first videophone that was affordable enough for almost everyone to have one in his or her home or office. It cost less than three hundred dollars for the telephone itself, and it didn't exactly allow real-time videoconferencing. Instead, it gave you a refreshed image on a tiny screen every second, which made it feel like you were looking at a montage of poor-quality still photographs.

Technology has dramatically altered the landscape for teleconferencing and videoconferencing. Today, if you want to have a telephone conference call, you simply call your local telephone company and set one up. The operator will give you a number to call and a code that will allow you to access the conference call. Almost any number of people can join the call for as little as twenty-five dollars per call (depending on the time and number of participants). The call is simply added to your telephone bill. Or you can use software to go through the Internet and set up your own teleconference.

There are plenty of options when it comes to videoconferencing as well:

Buy software. Several manufacturers have created software that will allow you to do real-time video- and teleconferencing over the Internet. One example is Microsoft's NetMeeting. You can also use the software's Whiteboard, which lets you collaborate in real time with others using graphic information and chat via text messages with as many people as necessary. According to Microsoft, companies like Boeing, Ford Motor Company, and Toys "R" Us use NetMeeting to communicate between divisions and do training.

Use a third-party company to set up the call. Companies like MeetingPlace.net will allow you to schedule and attend video and audio meetings. If you'd like to have regular video or audio conferences with several people across the country (or world), you can purchase a license for each of these individuals and hold unlimited conferences. The cost for voice and Web conferencing runs from ten to thirty-five cents per minute. Licenses for unlimited conferences start at $125 for a small group of users and falls to less than $40 per user if a thousand licenses are purchased.

Purchase your own equipment. Some companies, like Polycom Worldwide and Sony, will sell you all the equipment you need to create your own videoconferencing platform. You can use existing software and off-the-shelf components, or you can have a system custom-designed for your needs. Off-the-shelf parts and software can cost a few thousand dollars per set up, plus telephone line charges (which include a set-up fee that can cost another few thousand dollars and a small monthly fee). Designing your own video- or teleconferencing center can cost upwards of forty thousand dollars per location, plus several thousand dollars more to run it. If the videoconferencing unit isn't self-contained, you may have to hire someone to run the system.

Go somewhere. If you're a small business, you might not want to invest in video- or teleconferencing equipment. Depending on where your office is located, you could use someone else's facilities. Kinko's (the national copy center chain) has videoconferencing facilities. They work pretty well:

you go to a local Kinko's and the person with whom you want to conference goes to another Kinko's. The cost runs $150 per hour for each Kinko's videoconferencing center you use. If you're near a major university, you might ask if they have a videoconferencing facility and if they'd be willing to rent it out when it's not in use.

How Much Will You Use It?

There's no doubt that the technology of today and tomorrow can save your company a bundle in travel expenses. If you need to get four people from across the country together for a one-hour meeting, you could spend four thousand to ten thousand dollars on airfare, hotels, and other expenses, not to mention the lost time. A four-way video conference call at Kinko's will cost around six hundred dollars.

It all sounds easy, and the cost savings can be significant. The real question to ask is how much will you use this technology? If you're not sure how often your office would use videoconferencing, start small. Rent a videoconferencing center as often as you need it for a year. If after a year of using it on an as-needed basis you can detect cost savings and increased productivity, talk to a telecomm specialist about what it would take to install a system for your company.

Bonus Tip

If your boss needs to reach a much larger audience or you need the flexibility to rebroadcast a meeting, training session, or orientation session at various times, you may want to consider Webcasting rather than videoconferencing.

Videoconferencing happens in real time. It's like watching live TV. Webcasting can be live, but it can also be taped, posted to a Web site, and replayed as often as you like. Webcasts are easy to tape and far less expensive to produce than renting a videoconferencing facility. The downside is that there is about a nine- or ten-second delay with a Webcast (even if you use a T-1 line), and although those tuning in can participate via Webchat during the event, anyone who replays it won't have the interactivity. It's like watching a rerun of a television show.

30 Really Useful Tip

Use Software to Help Solve Everyday Problems

When you purchase a computer these days, it typically comes loaded with software. If you purchase a PC, you'll probably buy it with Microsoft Office installed. You'll probably never use most of this software, but if you spend some time playing around with it, you'll see that you have almost everything you need to make your office run right at your fingertips. If you're buying general software programs off the shelf, here are some basic types of software that might make your office life easier:

Word processing. Most of the world uses Word, which is Microsoft's word processing software. Whether you use Word or WordPerfect, word processing software lets you write, edit, design, and print letters, reports, and documents. With these programs, you can make changes to documents electronically, without having to rewrite everything.

Data management. It's helpful to have a place where you can put the contact information of your clients, vendors, associates, customers, and other people you connect with in your business and personal lives. Data management software should give you flexibility in sorting the names of these contacts, printing up labels, and even keeping a running log of activity. The top data management programs are Palm and Act!, although Microsoft Outlook does a fairly good job as well.

There is a software solution for almost any type of business issue or problem. At Quill.com, you'll find software for bar coding, AutoCAD design, mapping, labeling, clip art, development, digital imaging, education, financial management, Internet surfing, multimedia, operating systems, wireless networks, data management, productivity, tax solutions, Web site designing and hosting, training, and computer utilities. Quill.com also offers custom printing solutions. Click on "custom printing" for details.

Financial accounting. If you're running a business, you have to keep track of what comes in and what goes out. For small to medium-sized businesses, an off-the-shelf accounting program like Quicken, QuickBooks, or Microsoft Money is an easy way to track your income and expenses. At tax time, you can use off-the-shelf tax software and download your financials from your database. There are also Internet-based tax companies, like SurePayroll.com and Quicken.com, that will, for a small fee, prepare and electronically file all of the taxes you'll need to pay for your employees.

Presentations. Microsoft Office comes equipped with PowerPoint, which is software that generates a digital slideshow. It's extremely flexible and easy to use. How easy? In some classrooms, second and third graders use PowerPoint to prepare class presentations.

Security. If you're going to access the Internet, you'll need both antivirus software as well as firewall security software to keep your computer systems safe. Antivirus software prevents an electronic virus from infiltrating your hardware and crashing your system or stealing sensitive or private information. A firewall can keep your company network safe from hackers looking to control your system through an open Internet portal. The top creators of antivirus and firewall security systems are McAfee and Symantec Norton. The software is often on sale and is inexpensive, although you should sign up for the updates, which you'll eventually have to pay for.

Desktop publishing. Whether you're looking to produce a catalog, newsletter, brochure, form, or other document, a decent desktop publishing program will help you create a professional-quality product. You can purchase color printers, which are inexpensive, or you can go online to Kinkos.com and e-mail them your finished product to print for you.

31 Really Useful Tip

Learn How to Design and Update Your Company's Web Site

Pamela remembers the day she decided her company needed a Web site. She had just fielded a call from an exasperated potential customer who had spent about thirty minutes searching for the company's number on the Web. Since the customer didn't know what city Pamela's company was located in, it took a long time to find the number.

"If you just had a Web site, I could have found you in seconds," the customer told Pamela.

Welcome to the Web world. Today, it has become so easy to find people, companies, and products. The Internet has produced an incredible free exchange of ideas and information. The only companies that are left out are those that can't be found—or don't want to be found.

But your company is in business to sell something—or you'd be out of business. Whatever it is you're selling, prospective customers have to be able to find you. And once they find you, they might very well purchase what you're offering right on your Web site!

If your company doesn't have a Web site, you have to wonder why. You don't need anything particularly elaborate to get the job done. It could even be a one-page site that simply lists contact information for your company.

Getting Started

If you're going to put up a Web site, you'll need a domain name. My Web site is called ThinkGlink.com and Quill's Web site is Quill.com. If you go to any Web browser and type in ThinkGlink.com, my Web site will pop up. If you type in Quill.com, you'll go to Quill's home page.

You can buy a domain name for your site almost anywhere (think of these sites as retailers or resellers). But there is one central registrar for names, ICANN (Internet Corporation for Assigned Names and Numbers). Internic.net is ICANN's directory of domain name agents and it is as good a place as any to start your search for a domain name retailer. As an alternative, you can purchase a domain name through Yahoo.com, AOL.com, or Microsoft's MSN.com.

It costs about $35 to keep your Web site domain name registered every year with the federal government. Some domain name agents will offer you deals, such as register your domain name for ten years for $250 instead of $350. Why do they offer to do that? Because they're hoping that if you get your domain name from them, you'll also take advantage of their offer to give you a free Web page if they host the site.

These agents know you'll need a Web hosting service, and this is where they hope to make their money. So they think that if they subsidize your domain name, you'll stay there and allow them to host your Web site for you.

Web Hosting Services

A Web host is a company that provides the back-office power you'll need to deliver your Web site. The Web host owns a bunch of servers in a room somewhere, and one of them will make sure that your company's Web site appears flawlessly and consistently on the Internet.

You can get a free Web site from GeoCities, and Yahoo! will host it for less than $10 per month. Other sites claim to host Web pages for as little as $4.95 per month. America Online will create a free Web page for its customers (who currently pay about $24 per month for their service).

The real question is what kind of a Web site does your company need?

If you need to be able to take credit card payments over the Web, offer a thousand products, and provide hundreds of pages, you'll probably want to look into having a Web design company put together a custom site with all the bells and whistles. You may even buy servers and host the site yourself.

But if you can get away with something simple (for now), then you might as well take advantage of free or nearly free Web hosting services.

Building Your Site

There are thousands of companies that can help you construct a detailed Web site for your business. But you can probably put up something quick on your own in less than a day.

Software like Microsoft FrontPage (either the Express or current version) or PageBuilder allows you to create and format Web pages as if you were simply typing in Word. In fact, if you use FrontPage, once you set up your Web site you can easily upload text created in Word, because the program automatically formats it in HTML (a Web programming language). Using programs that work with Word allows everyone in your company to create pages of information that can be easily added to your site.

Each year, Microsoft upgrades FrontPage. Once you purchase the software, you can simply upgrade the product rather than purchasing new software all over again. You can purchase Microsoft FrontPage online from Quill.com.

Quill suggests

Make Your Site User-Friendly

When creating content for a Web site, make it easy for people to find what they're looking for. Here are a few suggestions:

Keep your Web presentation accessible and organized. If you're doing it yourself, keep it simple and easy to use. Don't go for gimmicks and goofy color schemes—think clean! A site map allows users to easily find the information they want. Put yourself in the customer's shoes: if you were a customer, what would you be looking for?

Put your contact information front and center. Well, it doesn't actually have to be in the center of the home page, but there should be a link that says "contact us," and that page should contain your company's name, address, phone and fax numbers, and other contact information.

Update your site as needed. If you simply put up a contact page, you probably don't need to change it too often. If you start putting up information that gets dated, you'll want to change or add to the content on a regular basis.

Invest in Web security. This is especially important if you're taking money over the Web or if you store sensitive information on your site. You'll want to use special software that will keep the information on your site secure. A Web design company can assist you in adding extra layers of Web security to prevent theft of sensitive information.

List your site with as many search engines as possible. That way, your customers will be able to find you. Look for search engines that focus on specific industries or geographic regions

Quill suggests

Web kits make Web site construction easy. Macmillan's Web Page Construction Kit 6.0 includes a user-friendly editing environment, ten thousand Web-ready graphics, an easy-to-understand manual, and other tools you can use to create a fabulous Web site quickly. See Quill.com for details.

with SearchEngineWatch.com. You should also list your site with Yahoo!, Netscape, AOL, MSN, Excite, Lycos, AltaVista, HotBot, Google, and Infoseek.

For More Information

There are more than a dozen books on putting together a Web site. Here are a few you can peruse at your local bookstore: *The Complete Idiot's Guide to Creating a Web Page, Designing Web Usability: The Practice of Simplicity, Microsoft FrontPage for Dummies, Web Design for Dummies, HTML 4 for Dummies,* and *Creating Web Pages All in One Desk Reference for Dummies.*

32 Really Useful Tip

Continue Your Computer Education

If you're going to be responsible for your company's technology, or if you just want to be more comfortable with computers and the Internet, you may want to continue your computer education.

The best places to do this are at local community colleges or your local university, where classes are scheduled in the evenings and on weekends to accommodate the schedules of those who work during the day.

You might also try some free online classes. These sites offer free courses, and they might be a good place to start your search for the right class:

- ✓ Intelinfo.com
- ✓ Freeskills.com
- ✓ Learnthat.com
- ✓ ActDen.com (Digital Educational Network)
- ✓ ComputersandTraining.com

Yahoo! and AOL also offer loads of free information on HTML and Java programming languages. You should also look for classes that offer the specific skills in which you're interested, such as learning how to use the latest version of FrontPage.

Internal Education

If you're lucky enough to have an IT department, ask if they can provide seminars on new technology from time to time. Or you might nominate one person in your department to be the technology contact. This colleague might read up on the latest developments and inform the rest of the department on anything of interest, or he or she may simply keep a file with tips on the technology and software your department uses. That way, if someone has a question, you'll know who to ask.

TOP TIPS
for Saving Money When Buying Technology

When it comes to technology, the longer you wait, the more you'll get for your money. At some point, you'll have to bite the bullet and actually purchase something. Since it will be outdated in a matter of months, you don't want to spend more than you have to. Here are a few suggestions for saving money when purchasing technology:

Shop around before you buy. Comparison shop—visit several (or maybe even a dozen, but not just one or two) suppliers before you plunk down your company's cash. Use the Internet to see what deals are being offered, and then try to break down those deals so you can compare prices on an apples-to-apples basis. You can also read consumer reviews at CNET.com.

Shop the sales. Most retailers offer discounts at various times of the year, or when a new product is being launched. Take your time so that you understand when something is really "on sale" and when it is a fake sale (more equipment than you need or the price has been pumped up).

Look for rebates and coupons. Quill.com offers coupons. Manufacturers offer rebates if you meet certain terms and conditions. I recently bought a seventeen-inch flat-screen monitor and received a $150 rebate, so it's worth seeing what coupons and rebates you can combine to get the best possible price.

Consider buying used or refurbished equipment from the manufacturer. Sometimes equipment doesn't work and gets returned to a company, where it is refurbished and then sold for less with a longer warranty. At Dell, for example, if you visit the site frequently enough, you'll eventually see that the computer you want has been returned and refurbished. Although you're taking a risk that it might be a lemon, just make sure the accompanying warranty will protect you.

Don't buy more technology than you need. For example, you may not need the top-of-the-line IBM ThinkPad. The entry-level or secondary-level version might be enough computing power for you and might save you thousands of dollars.

Don't upgrade unless there is a compelling reason to do so. Today's computers are so powerful that there is little need to upgrade every year if all you're doing is searching the Internet and word processing. Carefully analyze your needs before you whip out the company charge card and you might save a tremendous amount of cash.

CHAPTER 7

Managing Stress

Change: Anticipating It, Adjusting to It, Dealing with It

According to Dr. Steven Burns, change equals stress. That is, our bodies recognize anything outside our normal routine as a stressor, including getting a promotion at work or getting fired, buying or selling a house, or even having friends come to visit for the weekend. Based in southern California, Dr. Burns, who consults with companies about worker health and safety, says even "imagined change" can cause stress in the form of worrying about what will be.

As the song goes, "Que sera sera." What will be will be. And if we followed that advice in our daily lives, we'd be a whole lot less stressed out.

But that isn't how it works—at least for most of us. Change happens, and we need various amounts of time to anticipate it, adjust to it, and finally accept and deal with it. This is particularly true when change happens at work.

That's because most of us think of our jobs as being a stabilizing force in our lives. We have to be there every day during the same hours. Our tasks are fairly familiar, and while we may have a lot of them or even something new to accomplish, they typically fall within the bounds of what we do every day. For example, you might type a new document or order different supplies or make reservations to a new location for a business trip. But in essence, these are familiar tasks.

So when work does change, it's really rocks our world:

✓ The National Institute for Occupational Safety and Health reports that stress-related disorders are quickly becoming the number one reason for worker disability. The U.S. Bureau of Labor Statistics found that "neurotic reaction to stress" is the fourth disabling workplace injury.

✓ According to the Chicago-based International Survey Research Corporation, in 1988, 22 percent of workers said they frequently worried about losing their jobs. By 1996, that number climbed to 46 percent of workers polled.

✓ The National Institute for Occupational Safety and Health found that 25 percent of those surveyed said their job was the single greatest cause of stress in their life. Forty percent of worker turnover is due to job stress. Overall, job stress costs nearly three hundred billion annually in terms of absenteeism, diminished productivity, employee turnover, accidents, and medical, legal, and insurance fees.

On the landmark "Social Readjustment Rating Scale," created in 1967 by Thomas Holmes and Richard Rahe (first published in the *Journal of Psychosomatic Research*), the death of a spouse has a stress event rating of 100 (out of a possible 100) and getting divorced rates a 73. So getting divorced is 27 percent less stressful as the death of a spouse. (Although I know a bunch of divorced folks who would disagree with that!)

Getting fired rates a 47 on the scale. Working more than forty hours a week, having your business or work role change, or experiencing a change (positive or negative) in your financial life each rate a stress level of 38. Having an outstanding personal achievement rates a stress level of 28, and having trouble with your boss rates a 23.

The point of the scale is to show that stress factors (caused by positive and negative events in your life) add up over time and produce ripple effects that can have a powerful impact on your life. If you don't know how to adapt to and deal with change, the stress will eat you up inside and, over the years, turn you into an unhappy person.

In this chapter, I'll give you a few tools to help you deal with the stress you probably feel every day at the office. While some of these suggestions (like office Feng Shui) may seem a little exotic, just remember that they're working for someone, somewhere, in an office that probably looks a lot like yours.

33 Really Useful Tip

Take Frequent Breaks

According to the U.S. Department of Labor, half of all workers' compensation cases relate to repetitive stress injuries like carpal tunnel syndrome. In other words, if you do the same thing over and over again, hour after hour, day in and day out, you're not going to feel that great, and you could permanently injure yourself.

Colby used to spend long hours at his desk, staring at his computer screen for up to ten hours a day. As the administrative assistant for several executives, he was under the gun during his entire workday. He began to feel weak, exhausted, and nervous. His eyes were dry and bloodshot, his hands and wrists ached, and his back was sore. One day, he realized that his small aches and pains were going to grow into something much more serious if he didn't take some action.

What he did, successfully, was remap his entire workday. He worked out in the morning and took the stairs instead of the elevator when he got to work. During the day, he used the stairs to keep himself warmed up and pumped up. He took frequent breaks to stretch his back, do ten quick push-ups, and get fresh water. He brought fruit and vegetables to work and stopped eating a lot of heavy carbohydrates in the middle of the day. He used his lunch hour to take walks and limited himself to one cup of coffee per day.

Within two weeks, Colby had noticed a difference in the way he felt at work. Within a month, his bosses and coworkers had noticed it too and were asking him for tips on how they could adopt his newly positive outlook on life.

Colby had an extreme case of stress, which was causing him to be much less productive at work. But he's not alone. According to a new Xerox survey (completed with Harris Interactive), nearly half of all full-time office employees surveyed work nine to ten hours or more in a day but are at peak productivity for only half the day.

If you're at peak productivity for only half your day, it's hard to get everything done. Taking frequent short breaks can help. Stretching out your fingers, arms, neck, and back can help prevent repetitive stress injuries (and make you feel better), because you're giving your body something else to do for a while.

These breaks don't have to be long to be effective. For example, if you've been typing for half an hour and staring at a computer screen, take a minute to stretch out your fingers. Bend each wrist back and stretch your arms overhead. You might even want to stand up and stretch out your back. If your eyes feel tired from looking at small writing, look away from the screen or piece of paper and focus on something far away for thirty to sixty seconds. Walk to a window and look out. Take a bathroom break. Drink some water.

Take advantage of your lunch break by doing something physical. Walk briskly for half an hour, or if you have access to a gym and you have enough time, work out for fifteen, thirty, or even forty minutes, take a quick shower, and be back at your desk within an hour. Getting your body revved up will not only put you in better spirits, but it should also help you be more focused on your work that afternoon.

Check out Really Useful Tip #34 for some stretching exercises you can do at your desk.

34 Really Useful Tip

Exercise at Your Desk, during Breaks, or at Lunch

At the end of 2002, a *New York Times* article suggested that having a couple of glasses of wine would do your heart as much good as working out several times a week. Unfortunately, drinking isn't exactly an acceptable option for relieving stress at work.

On the other hand, exercise will not only help relieve stress but will also put you in a better mind-set to finish your shift. And if you have the kind of job where you sit at a desk typing for most of the day, a few easy stretches can work wonders.

At the annual meeting of the American Academy of Orthopaedic Surgeons in 1996, a team of doctors presented a study that suggested that a series of exercises could help prevent carpal tunnel syndrome (CTS), a repetitive stress injury. The exercises, which the surgeons suggested should be done at the start of each work shift and after each break, help decrease the nerve pressure that causes CTS.

The study found that a five-minute exercise warm-up before starting work, like a stretch before a run, would go a long way toward preventing injury for those with hand-intensive jobs, such as administrative assistants, barbers, keyboard operators, and bank tellers.

Hand and Wrist Exercise

Here is the easy hand and wrist exercise developed by the team of surgeons that can help prevent CTS. You should do this exercise before you start your job and after breaks. It takes about five to ten minutes to complete:

1. Raise your arms and flex your wrists. Your fingers should be pointing straight up. Hold for a count of five.
2. Straighten both wrists and relax fingers.
3. With your arms outstretched, make a tight fist with both hands.
4. Bend both wrists down while keeping the fist. Hold for a count of five.
5. Straighten both wrists and relax fingers. Count to five.
6. Repeat steps one through five a total of ten times.
7. Hang arms loosely at your sides and shake them out for a couple of seconds.

Back Stretch

When I started having back problems, I spent some time with a physical therapist, Steve Smith, who told me that I needed to take frequent breaks to stretch out my neck and back. He and personal trainer Monika Kocik-Markowski helped me learn these exercises, which are similar to exercises you will find at the Occupational Health and Safety Administration Web site, OSHA.gov. At your desk, you might try the following stretches:

Back stretch #1

1. Put your hands behind your head. Keep your elbows out to the side, over your shoulders.
2. Slowly relax your shoulders and pull your elbows back. Hold for a count of five. (You should feel the muscles between your shoulder blades come together.)
3. Slowly bring your elbows back to the starting position, then move them forward and try to bring your elbows together. Hold for a count of five.
4. Repeat several times.

Back stretch #2

1. Stand up.
2. Interlock your fingers and raise them over your head.
3. Stretch your arms toward the ceiling and hold for a count of five.
4. Slowly stretch your arms to the 10:00 position. Hold for a count of five.
5. Stretch your arms to the 2:00 position. Hold for a count of five.
6. Repeat as necessary.
7. Stretch your interlocked fingers in front of you and invert them so that you can see your knuckles.
8. Push out as far as possible. (Feel your back stretch out in a hump shape.)
9. Hold for a count of five.
10. Slowly release, and repeat as necessary.

Back stretch #3

1. Sit on the edge of your chair with your feet flat on the floor.
2. Firmly grip the back of your chair.
3. Lean forward so that your arms are straight.
4. Use your upper body to pull yourself forward to stretch your shoulders, chest, and upper back.
5. Hold for a count of five.
6. Slowly release.
7. Repeat as necessary.

Shoulder Stretch

If your shoulders aren't stretched out yet, you might try the following exercise that Steve Smith taught me:

1. Raise your shoulders.
2. Move them backward as far as they will go.
3. In a circular motion, bring your shoulders back to the starting position.
4. Repeat ten times.

If you have two bottles of water, you can add to this exercise. Stand up and grasp one bottle of water in each hand. Repeat the exercise twenty times.

Leg, Calf, and Ankle Stretch

Try these common exercises for achy legs. The first one is good to do on an airplane if you've been seated for a while. Monika taught me the second leg stretch, which I try to do once a week.

Leg stretch #1
1. Sit firmly on your chair.
2. Raise one leg out straight.
3. Flex your ankle so that your toes point straight up.
4. Push your ankle down, and point your toes.
5. Repeat ten times with the first leg.
6. Switch legs and repeat steps one through five.

Leg stretch #2
1. Go to the stairs and put the ball of one foot on one stair tread.
2. Hold on to the handrail.
3. Cross the other leg behind the first so that all of your weight is on the ball of the first foot.
4. Raise yourself as high as possible.
5. Lower yourself as low as possible (without falling off the stair tread).
6. Repeat fifteen times.
7. Change legs and repeat steps one through six. (You should feel your calf muscle stretch and contract.)

For More Information

There are loads of places on the Internet to get more exercises. Try these sites for easy stretches: www.backhealth.net and www.ivillage.com (type "keyboard yoga" into the search engine).

35 Really Useful Tip

Watch What You Eat

According to the Centers for Disease Control and Prevention (CDC), the number of overweight and obese adults in the U.S. rose dramatically from 1987 to 2000. Today, more than forty-five million Americans are obese (more than 20 percent above their target weight).

It's no surprise that many Americans have a weight issue: we put in long hours at our jobs (which are often desk-bound) and have busy lives that don't always allow for regular exercise. The third part of the equation is the easy access we have to junk and fast foods, which tend to be high in fat, salt, and calories.

If you read the papers or listen to the news, all this will sound familiar. What isn't talked about as often is the profound effect what you eat has on how you do your job and how you feel at different times during your workday. According to the American Dietetic Association, skipping meals or eating poorly can have a powerful impact on job performance.

Eating well means eating the right food in the right quantities throughout the day. Small, frequent meals give your body a steady supply of energy. That helps you work at your best pace throughout your shift. Skipping meals, as any nutritionist will tell you, will eventually sap your energy, making you sluggish and hungry. You may have difficulty staying focused on your work or staying awake at meetings.

If you're watching your weight, soup is one of the best things you can eat, says Monica, a registered dietitian. That's because most soups are low in fat. Eating something hot takes more time, allowing your body to feel full faster. You can purchase a package of fifteen Lipton Cup-A-Soups at Quill.com and keep them handy for quick afternoon snacks.

The Northwest Pennsylvania Diabetic Association and the American Diabetic Association teamed up to offer some "on-the-job" diet tips:

Breakfast

Eating something in the morning gets your body going. According to the American Dietetic Association, it boosts your metabolism (so you burn more calories in a day) and improves on-the-job performance because you feel more alert mentally.

The best breakfasts include low-fat proteins and some carbohydrates. Think eggs and toast, cereal and milk, fruit or juice, peanut butter on toast, cheese, or even a slice of pizza or a turkey sandwich. What doesn't work? Lots of sugary sweets (like the treats frequently found in office lunchrooms).

Lunch

According to the American Dietetic Association, eating a well-balanced lunch can help you avoid an afternoon slump. The good news is that these days, company cafeterias offer more healthy choices. Again, think low-fat proteins (yogurt or a turkey sandwich) and stay away from carbohydrates (like a big plate of pasta), which can make you sleepy.

Bringing your own lunch will not only help you eat well, but it will also save you money (unless your company subsidizes cafeteria food, in which case the cost might be about the same).

A good option is to bring your lunch and use a part of your lunch break to eat and the rest to go for a walk.

Snacks

Healthy choices, like fruit, crackers with a little peanut butter on them, or even a handful of nuts, will help stave off hunger pains and keep you going throughout the day. Again, stay away from sugary snacks. And if you have to have a coffee drink, ask for skim milk.

36 Really Useful Tip

Consider Office Yoga, Feng Shui, Meditation, and Massage

When it comes to relaxing at work, the goal is to make you more productive—not to put you to sleep!

While we've already talked about some of the more common things you can do, there are alternative relaxation therapies going on in many offices nationwide. While practicing Feng Shui may not exactly be your cup of tea, you could be leading office yoga classes before you know it.

Office Yoga

Yoga is a mind/body exercise. It was developed in India thousands of years ago and is often thought of as "meditation in motion." It consists of a series of stands and poses that focus on your agility and strength.

Yoga has become quite popular for several reasons: anyone of any age can do it, you don't need special equipment, and classes are reasonably priced. You'll find yoga classes at your local health club as well as at many park districts, hospitals (try the wellness center), and individual yoga studios.

These days, yoga is working its way into the office. Ellen is a yoga teacher based in northern California. She consults with companies and individuals and has created something called "desktop yoga," which involves strength and flexibility poses you can do at your desk during a five-minute break.

Therese, whose technology company is also based in northern California, says her company has actually brought in yoga instructors to lead classes at lunch in the company workout room. She likes that yoga is a fairly good workout but that you don't necessarily have to get "dripping wet all the time," which makes it easy to go right back to work.

For More Information

For information on yoga, simply type "desktop yoga" into your browser, or check out Diana Fairechild's book *Office Yoga*, as well as her Web site, www.flyana.com. Your local bookstore or library also should have a large selection of yoga titles.

Feng Shui

Feng Shui is the ancient Chinese science of harmonizing your environment with nature. Practiced widely in the Far East, Feng Shui has not only made its way to America, but it has become a respected form of home and office design.

Feng Shui masters say that you can harness the natural energy of the world (called "chi") and allow it to flow around you by the way you organize your home and furniture and by the colors you choose for your walls, carpet, and furnishings. Today, employees at many companies, including Microsoft and Coca-Cola, practice some form of Feng Shui.

According to Kirsten Lagatree, author of two books on Feng Shui, and prolific Feng Shui author Lillian Too, there are several things you can do to create harmony in your office:

Face front at all times. In your office or in meetings, sit so that you face the doorway or room entrance. Not being able to see who is coming can trigger "negative energy." If you can't look toward the entrance, place a mirror in front of you that can help you see the door.

Use ergonomically friendly computer equipment, including a curved keyboard, if possible. "Chi" flows better around curves.

Improve your workspace lighting. If possible, put light on the southern part of your desk.

Get rid of clutter. Clutter blocks "chi," Lagatree says.

Keep fresh flowers on the east side of your desk. Change the flowers when the leaves begin to yellow.

Avoid abstract art in your cubicle or office. Feng Shui experts recommend a mountain painting behind you (for support), a water feature in front of you (or one of those desktop fountains), and pictures or paintings of fruit on the east side.

For More Information

For more information on Feng Shui, check out www.ivillage.com, www.asiasource.org, many books by Lillian Too, including *Lillian Too's Little Book of Feng Shui at Work*, and books by Kirsten M. Lagatree *(Feng Shui: Arranging Your Home to Change Your Life* and *Feng Shui at Work: Arranging Your Work Space for Peak Performance and Maximum Profit)*.

Meditation

Meditation is a simple, but ancient, method of clearing your mind—some would call it a "no-mind" state. Those who practice meditation say it helps settle the mind and body by eliminating the stress, fears, and suffering we feel. It replaces these negative feelings with clear, calm energy.

Until you've done it a few times, emptying your mind can sound complicated. My son Alex will sometimes tell me that he can't fall asleep because he can't turn off his mind. It's just going and going and going. The easiest way I've found to empty my mind is to imagine a blank white wall. Don't let other thoughts crowd their way onto your blank wall. Just keep it blank, breathe in, and relax.

Meditation works well in an office setting because all you have to do is turn off the ringer on your phone, get comfortable (no, you don't have to sit in a lotus position), close your eyes, and empty your mind. After ten or fifteen minutes of imagining your blank white wall, you should feel completely refreshed.

Massage

Thirty years ago, a massage parlor sounded downright exotic. Today, it seems like every street corner has either a massage center that trains future massage therapists or a day spa that offers massage. Nearly every nice hotel has a spa that offers massage services, including the Grand Floridian at Walt Disney World.

But the real change has been in how business has embraced massage as a way to relieve stress in the office or work environment. When the Mortgage Bankers Association of America held its annual convention in Chicago, they hired a company to give five-minute massages to stressed-out lenders. A huge consulting company regularly hires a massage therapist to come into the office and do fifteen-minute individual massages. The company found that it raised morale and reduced tension for everyone in the office.

There are many different types of equipment and furniture that can help you feel good at your office. For example, the E. S. Robbins Feel-Good Chairmat contains hundreds of massage nodules to stimulate pressure points on your feet. Simply slip off your shoes and rub your feet against the pressure points to relieve tension. Find out more at Quill.com.

37 Really Useful Tip

Create Nap Rooms and Nursing Spaces for Working Moms

"You must sleep sometime between lunch and dinner, and no halfway measures. Take off your clothes and get into bed. That's what I always do. Don't think you will be doing less work because you sleep during the day. That's a foolish notion held by people who have no imaginations. You will be able to accomplish more. You get two days in one—well, at least one and a half."
—Winston Churchill

Have you ever felt so drowsy that you knew you couldn't do anything but close your eyes and sleep? Well, you're in good company. Napping enthusiasts include Albert Einstein, Napoleon Bonaparte, Thomas Edison, and at least three presidents: John F. Kennedy, Ronald Reagan, and Bill Clinton.

Over the years, sleep researchers have shown that a twenty-minute nap in the afternoon recharges your batteries and helps you be more productive during the day. Dr. James Maas, a psychologist and sleep expert at Cornell University and author of the book *Power Sleep*, believes naps should be accorded the same level of acceptance as daily exercise.

Because companies now realize that a fifteen-minute nap can make their employees more productive, some have set up separate nap rooms. These private, quiet spaces (yes, some are transformed closets) allow employees to catch some shut-eye and then return to work a few minutes later.

An editing firm in Chicago not only has a nap space set aside for editors (who will sometimes work around the clock to get a project done), but a pool table as well. The president of the company believes that a quick nap or game of pool makes everyone feel better and more relaxed.

Dr. Maas writes that the best nap is one that lasts less than thirty minutes. Sleep researchers agree that once you sleep for longer than that, you enter a deep sleep. It's much more difficult to wake up from a deep sleep and it can interfere with your nighttime sleep.

Quill suggests

To avoid sleeping more than twenty minutes, use an alarm clock. If your company has a nap room, you might ask your boss or office manager to purchase a small alarm clock for all employees to use.

Nursing Spaces

As the benefits of breast milk have become more widely known, many mothers are choosing to breast-feed their children—even after going back to work.

Some companies are less than understanding. Ellen says she had to go into an empty office, shut the door, and close the blinds to find a private space in which to pump for her child. Some employees even have to use a bathroom stall.

But a few companies have chosen to give working mothers who nurse a private space. It may even be the nap room.

For working mothers, particularly those who have just returned from maternity leave, a nursing space can be a way to relieve some of the tension and stress they feel leaving their baby every day.

38 Really Useful Tip

Look into Flextime and Comp Time

April often stays late at work to finish a project. She sometimes has to come in early to get something ready for her boss, a busy executive who travels frequently. But far from complaining, April is happy to put in the extra time. She gets paid for her overtime or can take comp time to make up the difference.

Around her television station, people think Amy, a producer, just leaves whenever she wants to. Instead, she goes home to spend hours on her home computer doing research for various stories. "I get way more done at home than I do some days at the office," she said. The flexibility she has helps her focus. When she has to work overtime on a shoot, Amy accumulates the hours and then takes a comp day (typically on a Friday so that she can have a long weekend).

Although many employees still work nine to five, companies are beginning to realize that some employees work better from home and others need flexibility to help manage their home and office lives.

Flextime can take many forms, depending on the employee's situation:

✓ Matthew currently works a compressed workweek. He works four days of ten hours each, two at the office and two from home. As a single parent with two small children, he needs the flexibility to make sure everything goes smoothly at home.

✓ Anne, a magazine editor, worked three days a week at her office and two days at home. Although she had a hectic profession with never-ending deadlines, she made it work by being available by phone and e-mail all day. But it also helped her get to her children's soccer games and put dinner on the table.

✓ Sarah's company allowed her to take a six-week maternity leave, followed by several weeks of part-time work before returning to full-time. Although she was home Thursdays and Fridays, she was available by phone if needed.

✓ Sally and Stephen agreed to split one job, commonly known as job sharing. One week Sally worked three days and Stephen worked the other two. The next week, they reversed the order. If one went on vacation, the other worked the full week.

Both flextime and comp time can help you eliminate stress in your life by helping you be more productive and giving you additional time off to rest and recharge your batteries. If your company doesn't currently offer flextime or comp time, talk to your boss, manager, or human resources department.

TOP TIPS
for Relieving Stress at the Office

According to a survey on the reasons for unscheduled absences from work, more employees are taking time off because of family issues, personal needs, and stress than because of personal illness. CCH, Inc., a business information publisher based in Riverwoods, Illinois, found that these three reasons accounted for 57 percent of the time taken off in 2002, compared to 33 percent for illness and 10 percent for entitlement (as in "I deserved it").

If you feel like you need a "mental-health day," as a third of those surveyed apparently did, try these tips for relieving stress at the office:

Try telecommuting regularly. Can you do your job elsewhere? Leonora, a bank attorney, works from home one or two days a month. She finds work time at home to be much more productive and says that the flexibility keeps her sane. "I don't feel like I'm on a treadmill as much."

Ask your boss about flextime. Can you work from 6:00 A.M. to 2:00 P.M.? Can you compress your workweek to four ten-hour days and take Fridays off? You won't know until you ask.

Make your lunch breaks count. Go for a walk. Do some office yoga. Meditate. See friends. Work out. Sit in the sunshine and read a gossip magazine. Don't just eat at your desk alone.

Stand up and stretch. Make sure you take regular breaks every thirty to sixty minutes to stretch. Warm up your arms and fingers before starting work to avoid repetitive stress injuries.

Drink plenty of water. Staying hydrated during the day is one way to keep your body functioning well. And don't rely on caffeine to give you a boost.

Make your commute count. If it takes you more than fifteen minutes to get to the office, try listening to a book on tape (or CD) in your car or on your headphones, reading a book, or organizing your day. You'll feel more productive when you walk through the office door.

Keep your work area clean. Clutter can stress your mind. Being organized is one way to make your day easier. For some great tips on how to organize your office, turn back to chapter 2.

Acknowledgments

For most of us, work is something we have to do to pay the bills. Coming up with easy solutions to tricky problems is how we get through the day. I am deeply grateful to the more than a hundred office managers, administrative assistants, secretaries, and other office personnel who gave us a few precious minutes to share valuable insights about what issues are important to them, what problems need to be solved in the office, and their "tricks of the trade" for coping.

Other experts who contributed their time include Hamilton Beazley (Beazley@gwu.edu), Eric Fraterman (CustomerFocus Consult.com), Pamela Harper (BusinessAdvance.com), Kathi Huntley (Knowledgism.com), Jason Jennings (Jennings-Solutions.com), Karen Jorgensen (JorgensenHR.com), Terri Levine (ComprehensiveCoachingU.com), Donald Nichols (don-nichols@hotmail.com), Lori Towers (Physicalkneed.com), Grace Walker, John Waskin (GetBillFree.com), Chris Widener (MadeForSuccess.com), Steve Smith (Schuldt Performance Center), and personal trainer Monika Kocik-Markowski (markosiek@hotmail.com).

Since Quill was founded in 1956, the company has built up a massive database of information, not to mention talent, in a variety of areas. I wish to thank the administrative assistants at the company headquarters in Lincolnshire, Illinois, who took the time to write thoughtful responses to my e-mails. Others, including Lynne Snyder, Ken Wnek, Carl Oberfranc, and Brian Preston, shared the wisdom they've gained from years of experience. Larry Morse and Kyle Anderson had the vision to provide quality information to Quill customers for free, and Laura

Tarsitano and Londa Della made sure every detail was in place. But this book would never have come to pass had Sarah Alter not said, "This sounds like a good idea." I am grateful for all of their input and support.

My assistants, Jennifer Catlin and April Powell, worked diligently, combing through mountains of research and calling everyone they knew in the trenches to get feedback as well as some of the best anecdotes used in this book. This was my first experience working with Heidi Hill, one of the best editors with whom I have ever had the pleasure to work, and I hope it won't be the last. She introduced me to e-editing, and I don't think I can ever go back. Heidi's team, which includes designer Patti Frey, has made the production process a joy. Jim Rooke, at Maple-Vail Book Manufacturing Group, kept the numbers coming and helped me through the process of publishing. And my thanks also go to my good friend Mitch Rogatz, publisher of Triumph Books, who helped me write my first book so many years ago and gave me the connections I needed to get this one across the finish line.

Finally, I am deeply grateful to my husband, Sam, the world's best real-estate attorney and editor, who continues to believe all my wildest dreams will come true.

Index

A

Act!, 160
ActDen.com, 168
ADSL (Asymmetric Digital Subscriber Line), 153–54
air filter, 128, 136
air freshener, 119
air quality, 128, 135–36
Alexander Hamilton Institute (AHI), 104
AltaVista, 167
Amazon.com, 66, 80
American Academy of Orthopaedic Surgeons, 180
American Diabetic Association, 185
American Dietetic Association, 184, 185
AmericanGreetings.com, 65
American Lighting Association, 132
America Online (AOL), 143, 164, 165, 167, 168
antivirus software, 161–62
Apple, 148
Association for Information and Image Management, 37–38
availability sign, 20
Avery, 65

B

backup disk, 52–53
    storing, 53
    See also CD-ROM; Iomega Zip disk
BarnesandNoble.com, 80
BlackBerry, 151–52
Bloomberg Financial, 119

Boeing, 157
boss
    communication problems with, 102
    difficult, 101–4, 116
    getting in touch with, 150–51
    improving productivity of, 99
    juggling the work of more than one, 17–18
    protecting from difficult customers, 78
    thanking, 106–8
brag board, 107
breaks
    exercising during, 180–83, 196
    importance of, 9, 127, 178–79
    keeping track of, 15
    to alleviate stress, 178–79, 196
Broadband Reports, 155
Burns, Steven, 175

C

calendars, 27
    electronic, 16, 55, 56, 152
    keeping organized, 16
Caller ID, 73
carpal tunnel syndrome (CTS), 126–27, 178, 180
    exercises to prevent, 180–81
CCH, Inc., 196
CD-ROM
    burner, 52
    for backing up files, 52–53
    storing, 53, 140
cell phone, 26, 145, 150–52
    using in the office, 110, 111, 139

Centers for Disease Control and
Prevention (CDC), 134, 184
chairs. *See* office furniture, chairs
CheeseandWine.com, 80
chi, 35, 188–89
Chicagogourmetsteaks.com, 80
chitchat
  as a time trap, 9, 16
  how to avoid, 9
Churchill, Winston, 191
citrusgifts.com, 80
client. *See* customer
clutter
  as a time trap, 10–11
  effects of, 35–36, 58, 197
  in office, 118, 189
  See also disorganization
CNET.com, 170
Coca-Cola, 188
colleague
  difficult, 6, 10, 89, 101–4
  thanking, 105–7
communication. *See* office
  communication
"Communication Competence and
  Business Success," 98
Compaq, 148
*Complete Idiot's Guide to Creating
  a Web Page, The*, 167
ComprehensiveCoachingU.com, 94
comp time, to alleviate stress,
  194–95
computer education, 168–69
  at the office, 169
  free online classes, 168
computer equipment
  cables and cords, 126
  computer, 124
  ergonomically friendly, 188
  monitor, 123, 124–26, 128
  mouse, 127
  printer, 146, 162
  software. *See* software

upgrading, 145–49
  See also technology,
  upgrading
computer files
  backing up, 49, 52–53, 54, 139
  naming, 50–52
  organizing, 49–54
  saving, 52–54
computer manufacturers. *See
  specific companies*
computer password, 139
ComputersandTraining.com, 168
computer screen. See computer
  equipment, monitor
conflicts. *See* office conflicts
contingency file, 39, 44
copyholder, 126
Cornell, 127, 131, 191
Costco, 152
coworker. *See* colleague
*Creating Web Pages All in One
  Desk Reference for Dummies*,
  167
crime. *See* office crime, tips for
  preventing
cross shredder, 140
cubicle etiquette, 109–11
customer
  handling complaints from, 74–75
  difficult, 76–78
  etiquette when dealing with,
  72–75
  feedback from, 64
  loyalty of, 71, 83–84
  purchasing gifts for, 79–83
  staying in touch with, 64, 65, 66,
  67, 85
customer base, cultivating, 63–67
customer service, 10, 61–62
  refining, 68–71
  representatives, 70–71
  tips for improving, 85–86
custom printing, 65

D

date file, 39, 55
defragmentation utility software, 54
Dell, 148, 171
Deloitte and Touche, 98
Designing Web Usability, 167
desks. *See* office furniture, desks
desk organizer, 124
desk safe, 140
desktop yoga, 188
difficult boss. *See* boss, difficult
difficult colleague. *See* colleague,
    difficult
digital cable modem, 154
disk utilities, 54
disorganization
    as a time trap, 10–11
    effects of, 35–36
    how to avoid, 11
domain name, 164
    agents, 164
    registering, 164
DSL (Digital Subscriber Line),
    153–54

E

eating on the job, 119
    breakfast, 185
    etiquette of, 110–11
    impact on job performance, 184
    lunch, 185–86
    snacks, 186
    tips for, 185–86
EddieBauer.com, 80
e-filing, 54
8.3 naming system, 50–52
    See also computer files, naming
electronic calendar. *See* calendar,
    electronic
electronic files. *See* computer files
electronic reminders, 55–56
e-mail
    etiquette, 74, 99

for keeping people in the loop,
    8, 24, 85, 99
free accounts, 53
printing, 54
saving, 54, 103
wireless, 151
emergencies, preparing office for,
    136–37
employee theft, 137
Employment Law Resource Center,
    104
energy levels. *See* personal energy
    levels
Epson, 65
ergonomic furniture, 121–28
    See also office furniture
ergonomics, 117, 125, 126–27, 131
    definition of, 117
    problems in office (quiz), 131
E. S. Robbins Feel-Good Chairmat,
    190
Evans, Jeffrey, 26–27
Excite, 167
"Executive Control of Cognitive
    Processes in Task Switching,"
    13, 26
exercise
    at work, 180–83, 187–88
    to alleviate stress, 180
    See also stretching
eyewash, 137

F

Fairechild, Diana, 188
Federal Trade Commission, 138
Feng Shui, 35, 177, 187, 188–89
Feng Shui, 189
Feng Shui at Work, 189
Ford Motor Company, 157
file chest, 140
file guide, 48
files
    coding, 45

disposing of, 47–48
protecting, 140
recycling, 48
shredding, 48
sorting, 45–46
See also computer files
filing, 37, 48
advanced tips, 43–48
dont's of, 47
electronic, 54
first level of, 39–40
filing cabinet, 41, 123, 124, 125
for flat files, 44
using out guide with, 44
filing system
building, 41
creating, 37–42
for oddly shaped items, 43–45
for projects, 22
organizing, 44–45
putting plan into action, 42
supplies needed, 41
types, 40–41
fire extinguisher, 136–37
"Fires and Infernos" log, 6
firewall security software, 161
first-aid kit, 136–37
flextime, to alleviate stress, 194–95, 196
Forbes, Malcolm, 105
Frango Mints, 106
Freeskills.com, 168
FrontPage. *See* Microsoft FrontPage
Fruit of the Month Club, 80

G

Gateway, 148
GeoCities, 165
Georgia Peach Basket, 83
gift certificates, 79, 80, 81, 82, 106
gift log, 79, 81
gifts
books, 80
cultural, 80
food, 80
for colleagues, 106–7
giving don'ts, 108
for customers, 79–84
giving don'ts, 81–82
giving dos, 82–83
for boss, 106–8
giving don'ts, 108
monogrammed, 79–80
office, 80
personal, 81
Godiva.com, 80
Google, 167
GrahamCheese.com, 80
grammar-check program, for e-mail, 74

H

Habitat for Humanity, 82
HammacherSchlemmer.com, 80
handheld computer, 16, 151–52
hand-holding
as a time trap, 10
how to avoid, 10
Handspring, 151
hanging file folder, 11, 22, 41, 43, 45, 47, 50
hard drive, defragging, 54
Harris Interactive, 179
HarryandDavid.com, 80
Hedge, Alan, 127
Hewitt Associates, 112
highlighters, 15
holiday party, 112
tips for running, 112–13
Holmes, Thomas, 176
Honeybaked.com, 80
HotBot, 167
HTML, 165, 168
HTML 4 for Dummies, 167
H2Oplus.com, 81
human resources department, 62, 94, 103, 104, 195

100-percent bar, to track progress of project, 24, 42
100 Questions Every First-Time Home Buyer Should Ask, 143

I
IBM, 148
IBM ThinkPad, 171
ICANN (Internet Corporation for Assigned Names and Numbers), 164
identity theft, 137
IKEA, 25
influencer, 65
Infoseek, 167
injuries. *See* office injuries
Intelinfo.com, 168
Internal Revenue Service, 70
International Association of Business Communicators (IABC), 98
International Survey Research Corporation, 176
Internet, 143–44, 170
    and networks, 148
    and teleconferencing, 156–57
    and videoconferencing, 156–58
    and Web sites, 163–65
    connecting to, 146, 153–55
    for backing up files, 52–53
    free calendar on, 55–56
    software for, 161
Internic.net, 164
interruptions
    as a time trap, 12
    how to avoid, 12
Intranet, 148
Iomega Zip disk, 140
    drives for, 52
    for backing up files, 52–53
Irving B. Harris Foundation, 119
ISDN (Integrated Services Digital Network), 154–55
IT department, 51, 54, 169

J
Java, 168
Jennings, Jason, 25–26
job sharing, 195
Journal of Psychosomatic Research, 176

K
Kelleher, Herb, 61–62
keyboard tray, 127
keyboard yoga, 183
keypad, 126
Kiesner, Fred, 28
Kinko's
    and videoconferencing, 157–58
    for printing projects, 162

L
label maker, 11, 41, 44, 45
Lagatree, Kirsten, 188–89
LandsEnd.com, 80
laptop, 52, 145–46, 149
leadership qualities, 90, 91–92
Learnthat.com, 168
Leo Burnett advertising agency, 119
Less Is More, 25
Levine, Terri, 93–94
lighting. *See* office lighting
Lighting Research Institute, 129–30
Lillian Too's Little Book of Feng Shui at Work, 189
long-term storage, 22, 37, 40, 41, 46
loyalty programs, 83
Lycos, 167

M
Maas, James, 191–92
Macmillan's Web Page Construction Kit 6.0, 166
Mac OS, 54
manila file folder, 22, 41, 47

Marketing Resource Alliance, 63
massage
  in the office, 190
  to alleviate stress, 190
Masterpiece Studio, 65
McAfee, 161
meditation, 189
  in the office, 189
  to alleviate stress, 189, 196
meetings
  as a time trap, 7–9, 99
  how to improve efficiency of,
    8–9
  planning in advance, 22
  scheduling, 31, 99
MeetingPlace.net, 157
Meyer, David, 26–27
MichiganBulbs.com, 80
Microsoft, 56, 157, 165, 188
Microsoft FrontPage, 165, 168
Microsoft FrontPage for Dummies,
  167
Microsoft Money, 161
Microsoft NetMeeting, 157
Microsoft Office, 160, 161
Microsoft Outlook, 56, 160
Microsoft PowerPoint, 160
Microsoft Scheduler, 23
Microsoft Word, 160, 165
monitor. *See* computer equipment,
  monitor
Mont Blanc, 80
Mortgage Bankers Association of
  America, 190
Motorola, 151
mouse. *See* computer equipment,
  mouse
MrsFields.com, 80
MSN.com, 164, 167
multitasking
  and productivity, 15, 25–27
  as a time trap, 13–14
  how to avoid, 14–15

N
nap room, 192
naps, health benefits of, 191–92
National Advisory Committee on
  Ergonomics, 117
National Council on Economic
  Education, 138
National Foundation for Credit
  Counseling, 138
National Institute for Occupational
  Safety and Health, 175–76
NeimanMarcus.com, 80
Netscape, 167
network, 49, 53, 147–48
  protecting, 161
New York Times, 180
Northwest Pennsylvania Diabetic
  Association, 185
Norton Utilities, 54
NOVA Group, 93
nursing space, 192–93

O
Occupational Safety and Health
  Administration (OSHA), 117,
  133, 181
office accidents. *See* office
  injuries
office bullying. *See* workplace
  bullying
office communication, steps for
  improving, 24, 98–100
office conflicts, 95–97
  causes of, 95–96
  steps for resolving, 96–97
office crime, 137
  tips for preventing, 139–40
office design, 118
  holistic, 118–19
  See also Feng Shui
office etiquette, 74
office furniture, 121–28
  backrests, 123

chairs, 121–23
desks, 122, 123–24
and computer monitor, 124–26
footrests, 122, 123
See also file cabinet
office injuries
causes of, 133–34
how to prevent, 134–35, 136–37
See also air quality; repetitive
stress injuries; stress
office lighting, 118, 135
tips for adjusting, 130, 132, 189
types of, 129–30
office morale, 92–94
tips for improving, 94, 189
Office of Health and Safety, 134–35
office safety, 133–37
office security, 137–40
office supplies. *See specific supplies*
office yoga, 187–88, 196
Office Yoga, 188
Ohio Industrial Commission,
133–34
OmahaSteaks.com, 80
organization
energizing effects of, 35–36
importance of, 11, 31
tips for, 57–58
See also computer files, organizing;
filing system, organizing
out guide, 44
overscheduling
as a time trap, 13
how to avoid, 14–15
to increase productivity, 30
overtime, 31, 194

P

PageBuilder, 165
pager, 151
Palm handheld, 55, 123, 145, 151,
152
Parade magazine, 99
password. *See* computer password

PDA. *See* handheld computer
perfectionism, 28–29
personal energy levels, 14–15, 23,
30
Polycom Worldwide, 157
PotteryBarn.com, 81
PowerPoint. *See* Microsoft
PowerPoint
Power Sleep, 192
prepaid phone card, 152
Press, Joel, 118
Preston, Brian, 134
printer. *See* computer equipment,
printer
prioritizing, 17–18, 30
procrastination
as a time trap, 12–13
how to avoid, 13
productivity, 25–26, 31
effect of breaks on, 179
effect of conflicts on, 95
effect of ergonomics on, 121
effect of flextime and comp time
on, 195
effect of lighting on, 130
effect of multitasking on, 26–27
effect of napping on, 191–92
effect of office environment on,
109, 117–19
effect of stress on, 176
effect of upgrading technology
on, 145
improving, 99
peak, 179

Q

QuickBooks, 161
Quicken, 161
Quicken.com, 161
Quill.com, 170

R

Rahe, Richard, 176
referrals, 65, 83, 86

Rehabilitation Institute of Chicago, 118
repetitive stress injuries, 178, 179, 180, 196
Rubinstein, Joshua, 14, 26–27

S
Sam's Club, 80, 136, 152
saying no, 19–20
  ways of, 20
saying thank you
  to boss, 106–8
  to colleagues, 65, 77, 82, 105–7
  to customers, 79, 83–84
screen cleaner, 125
screen filter, 126
screen glare, 126, 129–30
SDSL (Symmetric Digital Subscriber Line), 154
SearchEngineWatch.com, 167
security cabinet, 140
Sees.com, 80
sensory office design. *See* office design, holistic
SharperImage.com, 80
site map, 166
"Social Readjustment Rating Scale," 176
software, 160–62
  data management, 160
  desktop publishing, 162
  financial accounting, 161
  for presentations, 161
  for preparing taxes, 161
  for teleconferencing, 156
  for videoconferencing, 157
  for Web site designing, 165–66
  for wireless handhelds, 151–52
  project management, 23
  security, 54, 161–62, 166
  upgrading, 146
  word processing, 160
  See also antivirus software;
    defragmentation utility

software; firewall security software; *specific programs*
SOHO (Small Office Home Office), 154
Sony, 157
Southwest Airlines, 25, 61–62, 63
speakerphone, in cubicle setting, 110
spell-check program, for e-mail, 74, 99
SteaksandSeafood.com, 80
stress, 175–77
  as cause of office conflicts, 95–96
  brought on by financial troubles, 138
  tips for relieving, 196–97
stress event rating, 176
stress-related disorders, 175–76
stretching
  back, 181–82
  hands and wrists, 181
  legs, calves, and ankles, 183
  shoulders, 182–83
  to alleviate stress, 179, 180–83, 196
success board, 107
SurePayroll.com, 161
Symantec Norton, 161

T
T-1 line, 154, 155, 159
T-3 line, 155
technology, 143–44
  customizing, 146, 149
  tips for saving money on, 170–71
  upgrading, 145–49, 171
  used or refurbished, 170–71
telecommuting, to alleviate stress, 196
teleconferencing, 156–57
telephone etiquette, 72–73
telephone headset, 18, 110, 124

TheCookieCutters.com, 80
three-cut file folders, 44–45
three-ring binder, for files, 44
tickler file, 39, 41
Tiffany's, 80
time-management tips, 30–31
time-stamping, 45
time traps, 7–16, 27, 99
  finding in one's workday, 15
  keeping a daily log of, 15–16, 27
  See also chitchat; clutter;
    disorganization; hand-holding;
    interruptions; meetings;
    multitasking; overscheduling;
    procrastination
Today Show, 66
Too, Lillian, 188–89
Toys "R" Us, 157

U
University of Michigan, 13
U.S. Bureau of Labor Statistics, 176
U.S. Department of Labor, 117,
    121, 122, 131, 132, 178

V
Vernon, Lillian, 71
videoconferencing, 156–59
videophone, 156
Virginia Tech University, 138

W
Wall Street Journal, 109, 119
Waskin, John, 137–38
Web. *See* Internet
Web browser, 164
Webcasting, 159
Webchat, 159
Web Design for Dummies, 167

Web hosting services, 164–65
Web kit, 166
Web site
  books on building, 167
  building, 163–67
  creating content for, 166
  designing, 166
  free, 165
  listing with search engines,
    166–67
  security for, 166
  updating, 166
WGN-TV (Chicago), 105
"Whale, The," 127
white noise, 118
WilliamsSonoma.com, 80
Windows, 54
wireless handheld, 151–52
Wnek, Ken, 86
Word. *See* Microsoft Word
WordPerfect, 160
workplace bullying, 104
work, types of, 21
Work Yourself Happy, 94
World Trade Center terrorist
    attacks, 61, 136
wrist rest, 126–27

X
Xerox, 179

Y
Yahoo!, 53, 55, 164, 165, 167, 168
yoga, 187–88
  See also office yoga

Z
Zip disk. *See* Iomega Zip disk

About the Author

ILYCE R. GLINK is an award-winning, nationally syndicated columnist, television reporter, radio talk show host, and best-selling author.

Millions of people coast to coast read her weekly real-estate column, "Real Estate Matters," and see her financial news reports on Superstation WGN-TV. She is a talk show host for WSB-AM, in Atlanta, where she fills in for the *Clark Howard Show*. She also contributes commentaries to *Sound Money*, on National Public Radio. She has hosted her own nationally syndicated radio talk shows and has been the money expert for national television programs, including *Lifetime Live*. The hundreds of radio and television programs she has appeared on include the *Today Show, Oprah*, CNN, and CNBC.

She is the author of many books, including the best-selling *100 Questions Every First-Time Home Buyer Should Ask, 100 Questions Every Home Seller Should Ask, 50 Simple Things You Can Do to Improve Your Personal Finances, 50 Simple Steps You Can Take to Disaster-Proof Your Finances, 10 Steps to Home Ownership*, and *100 Questions You Should Ask about Your Personal Finances*. Her newest book is *50 Simple Steps You Can Take to Sell Your Home Faster and for More Money in Any Market*.

Ms. Glink has won numerous awards, including Best Consumer Reporter, from the National Association of Real Estate Editors, and the first Money$mart award from the Federal Reserve Bank of Chicago. You can visit her online at ThinkGlink.com.